FOUNDATIONS OF MUSIC EDUCATION SERIES
Allen P. Britton, Editor

Tests and
Measurements
in Music

Prentice-Hall International, Inc., *London*
Prentice-Hall of Australia, Pty. Ltd., *Sydney*
Prentice-Hall of Canada, Ltd., *Toronto*
Prentice-Hall of India Private Ltd., *New Delhi*
Prentice-Hall of Japan, Inc., *Tokyo*

Tests and Measurements in Music

PAUL R. LEHMAN

University of Kentucky

PRENTICE-HALL, INC., *Englewood Cliffs, New Jersey*

153.94
L523

Foreword

The practical aim of the Foundations of Music Education Series is to provide music educators with a unified but highly flexible and completely authoritative treatment of the most important professional concerns. Individual books of the series may be combined in various ways to form complete textbooks for the wide variety of courses in music education offered by colleges and universities across the nation. On the other hand, each volume has been designed to stand alone as a definitive treatment of its particular subject area.

The pedagogical aim of the series is to present practical and proven techniques of successful teaching in compact and readable form for both college students preparing to teach and experienced teachers constantly searching for more efficient ways of thinking and teaching. The highest musical ideals must be accompanied by the greatest amount of practical common sense if music instruction is to be most successful.

The aesthetic aim of the series is to emphasize the purely musical values that must be realized in any program of music instruction if that program is to achieve ends worthy of the time and effort required to carry it on. In short, each of these works assumes first of all that music must be true to itself if it is to continue to hold a respected place in American education. The most telling criticisms made of the school music program in recent years, almost all of which have dealt largely with alleged aesthetic failings, have written this lesson in letters large enough for all to read.

Last, having pointed out the unifying concepts that underlie the works in this series, it is perhaps equally important to emphasize that each of the authors has written the book that he wanted to write, the book that he believed would be of most value to the profession. The series encompasses the individual convictions of a great variety of the most highly competent and experienced music educators. On their behalf as well as on my own, may I express the hope that it will contribute in a practical way to the improvement of music teaching.

ALLEN P. BRITTON,
EDITOR

Preface

It is not entirely coincidental that this volume bears the same title as Jacob Kwalwasser's notable pioneering work of 1927. At that time Kwalwasser undertook to discuss the principles of aptitude and achievement testing as applied to music, summarize the current status of music testing, and survey the existing published tests in music. The purposes of the present book are essentially the same, although expanded to include examination of certain broader aspects of the evaluative processes in music.

In 1927 there were only a handful of music tests. The research literature concerning those tests was rapidly increasing, but it had not begun to approach the vast proportions it was to attain in the 1930's and later. The Seashore battery had been published only eight years earlier, and the Eastman experiment was but two years old.

A great deal has happened since. Today, what was earlier known as "the testing movement" is seen in a different perspective. We like to believe that we have a deeper insight into both the potentials and the limitations of music testing than had our colleagues of the 1920's. In view of the remarkable proliferation of music tests, the sizable increase in the research literature, and the modifications in the philosophic approach of music teachers to testing in recent years, there appears to be a clear need for a book similar to Kwalwasser's in orientation but new in content.

The term "test" is used here in its broadest sense. It refers to a series of questions or exercises designed to measure the skill, knowledge, capacity, achievement, or ability of an individual or a group. "Measurement" refers to the act or process of ascertaining the quantity, extent, or degree of a personal trait or accomplishment. In modern educational terminology, "measurement" has been largely superseded by "evaluation," which implies a value judgment beyond an ordinary quantitative determination. Although this book is concerned primarily with written tests of aptitude and achievement, it also includes some discussion of subjective, non-verbal evaluations in music. Regardless of the nature of the data or how they are obtained, it is their skillful interpretation that is the key to the entire process of measurement.

This book is intended as an introductory text for undergraduate or graduate students, though it may also prove useful to the practicing music teacher. It is not definitive in any sense. For comprehensive background information or complete explanations of technical terms, the reader should consult the more specialized works listed among the references.

Paul R. Lehman

Contents

1

Introduction

Can you connect these nine dots with four straight lines without removing your pencil from the paper and without going back over any of the lines? [1]

```
•    •    •


•    •    •


•    •    •
```

This test was devised by a Soviet professor to identify promising researchers. The rationale underlying the problem is that to arrive at a solution one must avoid assuming any limitations beyond those stated. Presumably, the student with originality and imagination not only will solve this problem quickly but will apply these attributes to the successful solution of more sophisticated problems.

[1] Used by permission. London Express Service.

Many of us, no doubt, would be reluctant to entrust the determination of our professional careers to so brief and unproved an evaluative device. Although the test may appear to some to have what is known as face validity, its reliability is adversely affected by its extreme brevity. Further, the person who is experienced in working such puzzles very likely will have a distinct advantage over the person who is not. Nevertheless, even this simple test is probably a better method of choosing students than picking them at random.[2]

THE NEED
FOR EVALUATION

Each of us spends a part of each day in making evaluations. Some of these are carefully and deliberately made; others may be hasty and possibly invalid. Sometimes one does not even realize that he is making evaluations. Nevertheless, he continuously evaluates and re-evaluates his job, his peers, his superiors, his automobile, the gasoline it uses, the behavior of his children, the meals he eats, and the news he reads in his newspaper. He evaluates every item he purchases, as well as every service that is performed for him, and he evaluates a wide variety of situations, objects, and impressions with which he is confronted daily. Rational behavior is based upon the evaluation of the likely outcomes of various possible courses of action viewed in the light of past experiences.

Making evaluations is an important aspect of the job of the teacher. To aid him in making these evaluations, he frequently utilizes tests and other measuring devices. The purposes of evaluation in education include the following:

1. Appraisal of Student Progress. The educational progress of the student is a matter of considerable interest to all concerned. In most teaching situations, particularly in secondary schools, the instructor must assign marks or grades at the conclusion of each grading period. Although the procedures by which the evaluation is accomplished and the uses made of the grades are sometimes open to question, the function is a necessary one and is likely to continue until a better system is devised.

2. Identification and Guidance of Talented Students. Knowledge of a student's strengths and weaknesses is an essential guidance tool. Such knowledge implies evaluation. The identification and guidance of talented students who could profit from specialized instruction are particularly important functions of evaluation in the field of music.

3. Appraisal of the Effectiveness of the Teacher. When a teacher evaluates a student, he also evaluates himself. If the student has not learned, it is fallacious to say that the teacher has taught. It would be unrealistic to expect every student to learn all that is presented to him, but the conscientious teacher will always be concerned with the quality of his instruction. One way to evaluate instruction is to evaluate the students who

[2] The solution is at the end of this chapter.

have received it. There is increasing emphasis today on the improvement of teaching as one of the major goals of testing.

4. *Appraisal of the Educational Process.* Expenditures for education are increasing rapidly. Schools are demanding and receiving more funds, better-trained teachers, and more complex educational media. As legislators recognize and respond to these needs, the public is justified in asking whether it is getting its money's worth. Tests designed to determine whether or not the students as a group are learning what they should be learning may provide an answer. Disregarding the difficulties involved in determining what it is that they should be learning and constructing tests to measure the extent of that learning, the approach is a legitimate one. Without evidence to indicate what is being learned or not being learned, important issues may be decided on the basis of narrow personal views or journalistic sensationalism.

5. *Motivation of Student Learning.* The awareness that an evaluation is imminent can be a powerful source of motivation for the student. Contemporary learning theory suggests that finding suitable rewards for positive behavior is preferable to administering punishment for negative behavior. The recognition that comes from doing well on an examination should be as powerful a motivating force as the fear of embarrassment associated with doing poorly. Although a high test score ought not to become, in itself, the student's primary goal, a succession of scores showing steady improvement can help the student realize that he is making progress.

6. *Establishment and Maintenance of Standards.* Scholastic standards cannot be set arbitrarily by teachers or administrators but must be related to the actual accomplishment of the students as reflected by suitable measures. Once standards have been established, the teacher can determine by means of testing whether or not they are being maintained.

7. *Evaluation of the Results of Research.* Education is increasingly concerned with research, and much of this research is of an experimental nature. Evaluation is basic to all such research. The experimenter who designs new techniques or materials can arrive at no conclusion as to the success or failure of his techniques or materials unless he evaluates the results they produce with respect to the results produced by conventional techniques or materials. Frequently, the evaluative procedures he uses have considerable bearing on the outcomes of his experiment.

THE NEED
FOR QUANTIFICATION

Even though we accept the need for evaluation, the question remains: In what form should the results of evaluation be reported? In many studies it is most convenient if the results are quantified, or expressed quantitatively. This means simply that the results are expressed in numbers. It may be adequate for some purposes to say that John is a tall boy, that Mary is a bright girl, or that this class did better than that class on the examination. However, for other purposes it may be necessary to know how tall, how bright, or how much better.

Quantitative thinking has long been important in the sciences. More recently it has become important in education. Certain aspects of music instruction do not lend themselves readily to quantitative methods, but those that do are of sufficient importance that the music educator cannot afford to be unfamiliar with the basic techniques involved.

Quantitative measurements enable the experimenter to draw precise conclusions from his research. Suppose that a music teacher wanted to find whether his junior high students could learn more about musical form by means of experimental programed techniques supplemented by special recorded examples or by means of traditional techniques. He might teach one section using his experimental materials and another using conventional materials; then he can compare the results. But how are the results to be compared? Unless one group is far superior to the other, it is difficult to be certain that the teacher's personal judgment is valid. He can seek the aid of other judges, but he may find that they do not agree. If he is to make meaningful statements concerning his experiment, the teacher must first devise some way to quantify the achievement of his students. This may be done by using an objective test. Assuming that the experiment is soundly conceived and well carried out and that he applies the appropriate statistical methods, the investigator may justifiably claim that one of the two techniques produced better results and, further, that the chances are less than 5 in 100, for example, that such a result would have been obtained if no true difference existed.

Experimental results can be no more valid than the tests upon which they are based. Usually there are a number of limiting factors that must be taken into account in interpreting research findings, but interpretation without quantification becomes almost impossible due to the vagueness and confusion of the impressions involved. By quantifying his data the experimenter can state his conclusions precisely, can claim in terms of probability that his conclusions are unlikely to be due to chance, and can proceed with confidence on the basis of his findings. Further, he can modify some of the variables and repeat his experiment to learn more about the cause-and-effect relationships present. All of the functions of evaluation are fulfilled in a far more useful and meaningful way by means of quantification.

HISTORICAL BACKGROUND

Tests are as old as civilization itself. Tests of strength, as in combat, are among the earliest performance tests. Legends and fairy tales are filled with accounts of various kinds of tests, frequently tests in which the hero was required to demonstrate physical prowess or successfully solve a puzzle or riddle in order to achieve his aim. Written examinations similarly have a very long history. The Chinese Emperor Shun, whose reign ended in 2205 B.C., examined his officers every three years, and after three examinations they were either promoted or dismissed (24:8).[3]

From their beginnings in the twelfth century, European universities administered examinations as the basis for awarding degrees, and many aspects of current testing practices can be traced to the early universities. Testing for aptitude, however, is a much more recent development than testing for achievement. The movement is generally considered to have begun with Wilhelm Wundt, who established a psychological laboratory in Leipzig in 1879, and James McKeen Cattell, an American student of Wundt's. In Paris, Alfred Binet sought to devise an intelligence scale to measure children's innate capacity for learning. He was concerned with distinguishing between those who were incapable of learning and those who were merely lazy. Since 1905, when, in collaboration with Thomas Simon, he published his intelligence scale, mental tests, psychological tests, and aptitude tests have proliferated at an overwhelming rate.

Though there had been a few experimental tests earlier, the *Seashore Measures of Musical Talent*, published in 1919, was the first music test battery to gain wide recognition. It is a tribute to the insight and imagination of its author, who worked without benefit of precedent, that this remarkable battery has exerted such a strong influence on music education and that it has remained in use from 1919 to the present.

The period between the two world wars saw at least one new music test created annually. It was a period of intense interest in quantitative measurement in all fields, as is evidenced by the publication of such tests as the *Chapman-Toops Bricklayers' Test* (56:191) and the *Stiebeling-Worcester Chart for Diagnosing Defects in Buttonholes* (56:177). The development of achievement tests in music was hampered by a lack of agreement among music teachers as to what specifically should be taught in the music program. Nevertheless, a number of achievement tests were published, and some were standardized or partially standardized, that is, norms were provided and evidence of reliability and validity was furnished. The achievement tests of Beach, Kwalwasser, Kwalwasser and Ruch, Knuth, and Strouse date from this period. It was a time of heated debate among music teachers regarding the merits of the various tests and testing in general.

Since 1945 relatively few music tests have been published. The increasing cost of standardizing and publishing tests has been an important factor in limiting the quantity, but until recently there has also been a decline in interest on the part of music educators in standardized testing. Viewed from our present philosophical vantage point, however, recent tests have usually been more sophisticated and have tended to be based on more solid principles of educational and learning theory than many of the earlier ones, though some still fail to meet acceptable technical standards such as those outlined in the American Psychological Association's excellent booklet, *Standards for Educational and Psychological Tests and Manuals.*

[3] Reference works are cited by number. See the References section at the back of the book. Numbers to the right of the colon are page references.

Here is the answer to the puzzle on page 1:

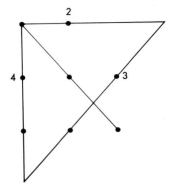

2

Musical Aptitude

The general lack of agreement as to what constitutes musical aptitude has been the source of much of the controversy surrounding its measurement. Writers on the subject, many of whom happen to be psychologists, have offered definitions differing widely in scope and complexity. At one extreme is the simple statement that musical talent is the ability to retain, recognize, and reproduce a short musical phrase (48:152). At the other extreme is Seashore's highly structured list of characteristic elements of the musical mind (52:7–8). Other authors emphasize the importance of absolute pitch, ability to recognize intervals, feeling for tonality, love of music, or general intelligence. Some suggest that such matters as will power, socio-economic background, and self-confidence may be relevant. Clearly, there can be no simple definition of musical talent. According to Seashore musicality is not a single talent but a hierarchy of talents, many of which are entirely independent of one another. Mursell, on the other hand, recognizes the existence of elements of musical talent but claims that there is a general factor of musicality common to all musical people.

Most tests of musical aptitude have been organized around certain elemental sensory capacities that the authors considered essential ingredients of musical talent. Seashore claimed that in his laboratory he could measure more than a hundred musical and non-musical characteristics that contributed to the musical talent of the individual. Not all of these capacities are equally important, and there are other important capacities that have been omitted because they could not be adequately tested. Specific capacities, such as the capacity to distinguish between two tones differing slightly in pitch, can be measured accurately, but complex capacities, such as the capacity to appreciate the emotional significance of a musical work, cannot be measured quantitatively. However, even in the latter case, we may measure certain of the factors which may be determining components.

Because musical talent is such a complex phenomenon, it is perhaps inevitable that experimenters should disagree as to the number and relative importance of its constituent elements. Intelligence could be measured before it could be defined. Apparently, the same is true of musical aptitude.

APTITUDE
AND ACHIEVEMENT

Traditionally, music tests have been assigned to one of two broad categories for convenience in classification. Those known as aptitude tests are designed to measure innate capacity for musical learning, even though no such learning may actually have taken place. Those known as achievement tests are designed to measure how much a student has accomplished in music or in a particular phase of music. An achievement test may attempt to measure facts, skills, appreciations, or other aspects of learning, but it measures only the extent to which the learning has taken place. It offers no specific insight into the ability of the individual for further learning.

Musical aptitude is usually defined as the potential or capacity for musical achievement. Most authors use the terms "musical aptitude," "musical talent," and "musicality" interchangeably. The term "musical ability," on the other hand, refers to musical powers or qualifications which may be either innate or acquired. "Ability" takes into account achievement while "aptitude" does not.

The concept of musical aptitude is a simple one, but designing a test to measure it is very difficult. By definition, aptitude is independent of achievement. Therefore, a test of aptitude must be constructed in such a way that the musical training an individual may or may not have received will in no way affect the result. Theoretically, a professional musician and a non-musician with the same innate capacity will receive the same score, even though the capacity of the latter is undeveloped due perhaps to lack of time, money, interest, or self-discipline. In practice it is almost impossible to determine whether this condition has been met, and the necessity to avoid the effects of training severely restricts the test author's choice of content.

Despite the amount of time and effort expended in developing tests of musical aptitude over the past half-century, the results have fallen considerably short of what many have desired. Part of the difficulty is due to the inability of either musicians or psychologists to agree on what constitutes musical talent, but part of the difficulty results from the seeming impossibility of disentangling aptitude from achievement.

In recent years psychologists have tended to believe that intelligence tests and other tests of special aptitudes, including music, do not actually measure innate capacity according to the rigid traditional definition of the term. They have recognized that musical achievement cannot help but have some effect on the results of an aptitude test. In practice we cannot entirely separate the results of aptitude from those of achievement, though we may continue to distinguish between the two for the sake of convenience.

Not only is it now accepted that achievement affects the measurement of aptitude, but it now appears that achievement can be an excellent indicator of aptitude. How can one measure the aptitude of a student for graduate work in music, for example? One convenient method would be to give him an achievement test to measure what he has accomplished as an undergraduate. The assumption is that he will probably continue to achieve at approximately the same rate. Viewed in this light the distinction between aptitude and achievement becomes blurred and indistinct. The two types of tests have descended from different historical traditions, but their functions now appear to overlap until the difference between them becomes one of purpose rather than content. A test devised to measure how much students have learned is called an achievement test although the results may depend partially on aptitude, while a test developed to select talented students is called an aptitude test even though the results may depend partially on training. The interrelationship between heredity and environment is so complex that no one has yet been able to distinguish adequately between the two, and at least some experimenters have given up trying.

TESTING FOR MUSICAL APTITUDE

There are a number of reasons why music educators have been concerned with testing for musical aptitude:

1. Identification of Talent. Tests can identify and encourage, at an early age, students with musical talent that might otherwise pass unrecognized and undeveloped.

2. Adaptation for Individual Differences. Tests can enable the teacher to set realistic musical goals for the untalented but eager student, challenging but not frustrating him.

3. Educational Guidance. Test results may be useful to the teacher in advising the student which instrument he should play or which musical activities he is best suited to participate in.

4. Vocational Guidance. Tests can provide valuable objective information for the student considering a career in music.

5. Discovery of Learning Difficulties. Tests can reveal and sometimes diagnose sensory or perceptual weaknesses or other learning difficulties that might otherwise go undetected; such defects may or may not be correctable, but awareness of their existence may result in the student's being assigned to another musical activity or being observed in a different light.

6. *Ability Grouping.* In schools organized on the basis of ability grouping, tests can assist the teacher in making such groupings.

7. *Assignment of Instruments.* Test results can be used to determine which students are to be assigned school-owned instruments when there are more applicants than instruments and when such a criterion is compatible with school policy.

8. *Studies of Musical Talent.* Tests may be useful to the psychologist by revealing the extent and distribution of musical talent and the magnitude of individual differences in talent.

9. *Psychological Studies.* Tests can aid in various psychological and genetic studies concerning, for example, the relationship between musical aptitude and intelligence, achievement, sex, race, or age.

Although aptitude tests have definite uses, they also have limitations, many of which arise either from the inability of teachers to interpret the results satisfactorily or from erroneous conceptions of the purposes of aptitude testing. Most authors of aptitude tests, aware of the possible consequences, have specifically warned against the misuse of their tests. Seashore, in particular, stressed that his battery was but one of many evaluative tools which, when used discriminatingly by a competent person, could be useful in predicting probable success. Much of the criticism that has been directed against Seashore has resulted from the failure of teachers to heed his warnings concerning the limitations of his battery. Aptitude tests alone cannot supply the final answers to important questions but serve only to aid the teacher in arriving at a judgment on the basis of all of the evidence available in the student's cumulative record. Tests are not infallible. The question is, to what extent is a given test an improvement over the unassisted judgment of the teacher? To what extent does it remove the judgment of the teacher, as Mursell puts it, "from the realm of guess into the realm of reasonable certainty"?

THE RELATIONSHIP
OF APTITUDE
TO OTHER TRAITS

There is a sizable body of literature which purports to investigate the differences in musical aptitude among various racial and national groups. A number of investigators have studied the aptitude of Negroes as compared with Caucasians, and others have studied the aptitude of Germans, Italians, British, Poles, Russians, Jews, Japanese, Mexicans, Eskimos, East Africans, American Indians, and others. Usually, one of the standardized tests of musical aptitude has served as the basis for the investigation. Examining this literature as a whole, the best one can say is that it is inconclusive. The findings are by no means in agreement. The studies comparing Negroes and whites, in particular, are strikingly contradictory. In most instances the small differences which were found may be attributable to the imperfect reliability and validity of the tests, the small size of the samples, or environmental factors on the part of the subjects. Similarly, studies investigating the relationship between musical aptitude and intelligence, age, sex, and motor skills have been largely inconclusive, but the majority of them have found no significant relationship.[1]

[1] For a summary of these studies, see 25:43-119.

3

Criteria
of a Good Test

Regardless of the limitations of his technical knowledge about testing, every educator should have a basic understanding of the criteria of a good test. Most of these criteria apply to teacher-made tests as well as to published standardized tests. They apply to all tests regardless of content field, length, level, or types of items included.

RELIABILITY

One important criterion is reliability. Reliability refers to the consistency with which a test measures. Suppose that a person were to take the same test twice and receive scores of 90 per cent and 20 per cent. He would conclude that the test is inconsistent and, therefore, unreliable. A reliable test will measure accurately, and one that measures accurately will be consistent if the characteristic being measured is consistent.

The Determination of Reliability

In order to determine the reliability of a test, the investigator must obtain two scores for each individual.

This is normally done in one of three ways:

1. *The Split-Half Method.* In determining reliability by the split-half method, the score for each person on half of the items is compared with his score on the other half of the items. Usually, the comparison is made between the score on the odd-numbered items and the score on the even-numbered items. The limitation of this method is that the examiner has, in effect, reduced the length of the test by one half, which in itself will tend to lower the reliability.

2. *The Equivalent-Forms Method.* The equivalent-forms method requires that the test-maker devise two forms of the test that are equivalent in every respect. The major drawback of the equivalent-forms method is the difficulty in being certain that the two forms are indeed equivalent. If a low reliability is obtained, the experimenter may be unable to determine the extent to which his test is actually unreliable and the extent to which the two forms are nonequivalent.

3. *The Test-Retest Method.* The third method, known as the test-retest method, requires that the same test be administered twice to the same group of individuals, with an intervening period of time. The principal limitation inherent in this method arises from the possibility that memory, maturation, or new learning experiences may affect the results on the second testing.

The Coefficient
of Reliability

Reliability is computed as the correlation r between the two sets of scores according to the formula given in Chapter 4. It is expressed as a coefficient of reliability, the statistical equivalent of the coefficient of correlation between the two sets of scores. The more closely the scores for each individual resemble one another, the more closely the reliability coefficient will approach a perfect 1.00.

How high should the reliability of a test be? Obviously, the higher the better. How low can it fall before the test becomes useless? Unfortunately, there can be no answer that will apply in all circumstances. A reliability of .85 is generally considered satisfactory, although it depends upon the nature of the test, the variability within the group, and the purposes for which the test is used. If a test is used to distinguish between individuals, it is desirable to have a reliability coefficient of at least .90, but for some group measurements reliabilities as low as .60 or even .50 may be useful. The situation is somewhat analogous to determining the tolerances necessary in the construction of a trumpet, where accuracy to the nearest .0001 in. may be required in fitting the valves, but errors of up to .01 in. might be acceptable at some points along the bore.

Factors Contributing
to Reliability

What makes a test reliable? There are a number of characteristics that contribute in varying degrees to the reliability of a test:

1. Length. Until the point is reached when fatigue affects the performance of the subject, the longer a test is the more reliable it will tend to be Luck and other chance factors tend to exert greater influence when there are only a few items, but the more items there are the more likely it is that the true ability of the student will be revealed.

2. Objectivity. The greater the extent to which the scoring of the test is independent of the personal viewpoints and interpretations of the scorer, the more reliable it will tend to be.

3. Heterogeneity of the Group. The wider the variance within the group tested, the more reliable the test will appear to be. If the differences in ability among the members of the group are slight, a few errors will have a greater effect on the rank order of the students than in a group where the differences in ability are great.

4. Clarity and Conciseness. The more clearly and concisely the directions and the test items are stated, the more reliable the test will tend to be.

5. Conditions of Administration. Favorable testing circumstances, such as sufficient light, proper temperature, adequate ventilation, comfortable seats, absence of distractions, and freedom from emotional disturbances, tend to result in higher test reliabilities than unfavorable circumstances. Similarly, when a test is given in typical and familiar surroundings, it is likely to yield a higher reliability than when it is given in unusual or unfamiliar surroundings.

6. Independence of Items. The reliability of a test will tend to be higher if each item is independent of the others. The alert student can sometimes figure out the answers to questions from information contained in other questions.

7. Order of Items. The arrangement of test items in progressive order of difficulty may tend to raise the reliability. If items are arranged at random, the student may become discouraged by finding very difficult items near the beginning of the test or he may waste time puzzling over questions he cannot answer.

8. Scope. The more limited the field covered by a test and the smaller the range of item difficulty, the more reliable the test will tend to be.

The effect of the scope of the test deserves special mention because of its relevance to music tests. Items that are decidedly too difficult or decidedly too easy are of no help in determining the limits of the individual's knowledge or skill. A test containing items representing a wide range of difficulty may be satisfactory for testing unselected samples of the population but unsatisfactory for testing specialized groups of persons with similar abilities. At the same time, a test containing items representing a narrow range of difficulty may be satisfactory for testing specialized groups but unsatisfactory for testing groups from the general population.

VALIDITY

Reassuring as it is to know that a test is accurate and consistent in its measurement, the results are nevertheless of little help in drawing conclusions about people until we know just what it is that the test measures. A good test must be valid. Validity refers to the extent to which a test actually measures what it claims to measure. If a test entitled *Smith Test of Sight Singing* contains mostly items dealing with instruments of the orchestra, history of music, and identification of composers, the teacher may conclude that it is invalid because it does not measure what it purports to measure. Validity, like reliability, is expressed in terms of a coefficient. If a test could measure perfectly what it claims to measure, it would be said to have a validity coefficient of 1.00. In practice, validity coefficients are never that high, and most are substantially lower.

Types of Validity

The concept of validity is a complex one. The shortcomings of a test with respect to validity are usually far more subtle than in the example cited. For one thing, there are several ways in which validity may be viewed:

1. *Face Validity*. Face validity refers to the extent to which, on the basis of a more or less superficial inspection, a test appears to the teacher or student to cover the material taught in the classroom. If a test covers the material he assumed or was told that it would cover, the student is likely to be more highly motivated than if it does not.

2. *Content Validity*. Content validity is similar to face validity but requires more detailed examination. To be valid in this sense, the test must contain a balanced, representative sampling of the content of the curriculum. Content validity is perhaps the most important type of validity in tests of achievement.

3. *Empirical Validity*. Empirical validity refers to the extent to which scores obtained on the test relate to given standards of performance or other criteria. If the empirical validity is high, the test can be used to predict performance on similar tasks in the future and may be said to possess predictive validity. Predictive validity is of critical importance in aptitude tests.

4. *Construct Validity*. Construct validity refers to the relationship between test scores and other criteria of behavior that logically should relate to the test. It is more concerned with theory and logic than is empirical validity.

5. *Formal Validity*. If the instructions are clear, the items unambiguous, and the papers of convenient size, type, and format, a test is said to possess formal validity. This characteristic of a test is not difficult to provide for, but its absence will considerably reduce the test's usefulness.

The Determination
of Validity

The most common methods of establishing validity are (1) comparison with a measure of known validity, (2) comparison with course grades or with the subjective ratings of competent judges, and (3) comparison with curricular criteria such as textbooks, courses of study, and lists of objectives.

All three methods, but particularly the first two, embody one apparent and crucial weakness: the criterion data themselves may be invalid. In utilizing a measure of "established" or "proved" validity, one should know how the validity was established or proved. It may have been by means of comparison with yet another measure. If so, the experimenter may find himself in a bog of statistical quicksand, unable to obtain a solid foothold from any existing criterion. Tests of musical aptitude are commonly validated against the Seashore battery, but the validity of the Seashore battery is still hotly contested.

Another difficulty with the second and third methods is that the investigator cannot begin with quantitative data but must derive his data from subjective evaluations. Studies have shown teachers' evaluations to be dependent upon a number of factors that limit their effectiveness as criteria for validating tests.

Reliability and validity are the two most important criteria of a good test. The educator should not, however, let the ordinary usage of the word "reliable" mislead him into thinking that a reliable test is good for any purpose. He must know just what it is that the test measures. A test may be reliable without being valid for the purpose he contemplates using it.

On the other hand, a test cannot be valid without being reliable also. It cannot measure anything satisfactorily unless it measures consistently and accurately. Statisticians usually consider that the validity of a test cannot be greater than the square root of its split-half reliability.

In selecting an aptitude test, the music educator must be particularly careful not to accept uncritically whatever may be offered him. It is a simple task to assemble a group of questions or exercises and label them an aptitude test. The title of a test may be completely misleading as to what the test actually evaluates. The teacher must ask himself what mental processes are represented by the scores obtained on the test and how closely these processes relate to the knowledge or skills he is seeking to evaluate.

There is no minimum validity coefficient that may be used universally to separate acceptable tests from unacceptable ones. A test cannot be considered valid in the abstract. It must be judged in the light of a specific purpose and under a specific set of circumstances. It must be judged in relation to similar tests under similar circumstances. Using an aptitude test of low validity would probably be an improvement over guessing, but whether or not the improvement would be sufficient to make the test worth giving depends upon the circumstances.

It is also important to remember that our understanding of the validity of a given test is constantly changing as more experimentation is undertaken. Validity is never a static thing. It evolves over a long period of time as examiners become more and more familiar with the test. The validity of an established test, such as the Seashore battery, is better understood with each passing year.

OTHER CRITERIA

In addition to reliability and validity, there are several other criteria of a good test. Some of these contribute to the two primary criteria. Some are of little importance in teacher-made tests, though of considerable importance in standardized tests:

1. Ease of Administration. A good test is easy to administer and score. It requires no unusual or complex apparatus. It may be scored quickly, perhaps by machine. Recorded tests are usually very easy to administer. If large numbers of persons are to be examined, a test that can be given to groups will be easier to administer than one that must be given individually.

2. Objectivity. A good test is objective. This means that each response is either correct or incorrect. The person scoring the test is not required to make value judgments, and the score of the student would be the same regardless of who scored the test from a given key. True-false, matching, and multiple-choice items are examples of objective items. Further, objectivity implies that experts would agree on the answer. To ask whether Beethoven was born in 1770 or 1870 is an objective item, but to ask whether his fifth symphony is greater than his third symphony is not truly an objective item even though it appears in an objective format.

3. Economy. A good test is economical of time and money. In large testing programs time and money often become important considerations. It is never wise to sacrifice reliability and validity for the sake of economy, but, in choosing between tests of similar reliability and validity, economy would be a legitimate criterion.

4. Standardization. A good test is well standardized. It includes published norms so that the teacher can compare the performance of his students with the performance of other students of the same age and grade level. Standardization also implies that evidence of reliability and validity is presented. Of course, this criterion does not apply to teacher-made tests.

5. Organization. A good test is well organized. The instructions are clear, complete, and concise. The format is clear and easy to read. The items are conveniently arranged in progressive order of difficulty, and they are well separated. If a music test is given from a recording, the recording states the number of each test item; otherwise, a student who becomes lost remains lost throughout that section.

A test in which speed is an important factor in determining the student's score is known as a speed test or a paced test. A test in which speed is not an important factor is known as a power test or maximum-performance test. Most music tests are power tests. Those including aural examples are paced in the sense that the class must proceed at the same rate, but the time allowed is usually sufficient for nearly every member of the group.

The teacher cannot expect to find a test that will be ideally suited to his needs. He must examine the available tests, weigh their relative merits, and make a judgment on the basis of his specific requirements. Above all, he must not let his high regard for a test cause him to use it in an evaluative role for which it is unsuited. The result may be serious misjudgment of his students.

4

Statistical
Concepts

Statistics deals with the collection, organization, analysis, and interpretation of quantitative data. An understanding of the basic principles of statistics is necessary for the educator if he is to read and interpret the literature in his field. This chapter is concerned with only the most elementary statistical concepts found in studies dealing with tests and measurements in music.

Statistical measures may be grouped under a series of broad categories. These include measures of central tendency, measures of variability, measures of relative position, measures of relationship, and measures of statistical reliability.

CENTRAL TENDENCY

If we were to measure the heights of a large number of men, we would find some that were relatively tall and some that were relatively short, but most of the values would tend to cluster around a midpoint. If we were to construct a graph showing the number of individuals of each height, we might obtain a curve similar to that in Fig. 4-1.

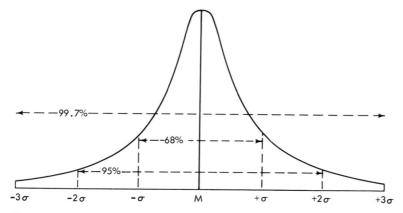

Figure 4-1. Normal probability curve.

In dealing with large samples from the general population, many physical or mental traits are found to have distributions that resemble the curve of Fig. 4-1, which is variously known as a bell curve, normal distribution curve, normal probability curve, or Gaussian curve.

The most common of the statistical measures used in describing this phenomenon of central tendency is the *mean*. The mean is simply an arithmetical average. It is arrived at by adding together all of the measurements and dividing by the total number of cases. The formula for computing the mean is

$$M = \frac{\Sigma X}{N},$$

where M is the mean, N is the number of cases, X is the individual score, and Σ (upper-case Greek sigma) means "the sum of." ΣX, therefore, means "the sum of all the scores." The mean fluctuates very little with variations in sampling.

Another widely used measure of central tendency is the *median (Md)*. The median is the point on either side of which half of the measures lie. It is found by counting half of the cases from either the top or the bottom and, if necessary, interpolating within the middle interval. If we line up 99 men according to height, the height of the fiftieth man will be the median for the group.

The median is used when there are extreme cases at the high or low ends of the distribution and the investigator, while concerned with their presence, is not particularly concerned with how high or how low they are. The mean is recommended for most serious research projects, but the median is convenient and adequate for crude statistical work or for work with small samples. Suppose, for example, that a sociologically minded director is studying the incomes of the families of the members of his horn section and that those incomes happen to be $7,000, $8,500, $9,800, and $300,000.

The mean is $81,325, but such a figure reveals little about the true central tendency within the group. The median, $9,150, would be a much more meaningful indicator.

In a symmetrical curve, as in Fig. 4-1, the mean and the median will coincide. However, if the curve is asymmetrical, or skewed, as in Fig. 4-2, the two will differ. The distribution in Fig. 4-2 is skewed positively, or to the right, and the mean will be higher than the median. If it were skewed negatively, the mean would be lower than the median.

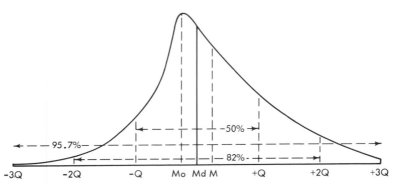

Figure 4-2. Distribution skewed positively.

The *mode* (*Mo*) is the score made by the largest number of individuals. It is determined by inspection of the raw scores. A distribution that has two separate peaks is said to be bimodal. The mode is less widely used than either the mean or the median.

Although the term "average" is sometimes used synonymously with mean, all three measures of central tendency are averages in the sense that they are measures of the performances of the average individual. "Average" has no technical meaning and should not be used except generically.

VARIABILITY

Suppose that the distributions in Fig. 4-3 represent the test scores of two sections of a ninth-grade general music class. The two distributions have the same mean, but the curves reveal striking differences between the groups. One group (A) is much more heterogeneous than the other (B) and would require greater variety in teaching materials and techniques.

To describe the differences between the two distributions, we need to know more than the mean or median. We also need a measure of the variability, or dispersion, within the groups. The simplest such measure is the *range*. The range is the spread between the highest and lowest scores. If the lowest score on a test is 33 and the highest is 96, we say that the range is from 33 to 96. As a statistical measure, however, the range is unsatisfac-

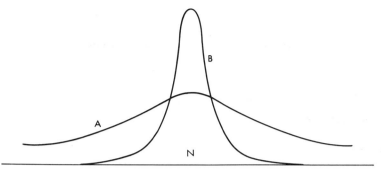

Figure 4-3. Two distributions of the same area (N) and mean but of very different variability. (From Henry E. Garrett, Statistics in Psychology and Education, 5th ed. New York: David McKay Co., Inc., 1958), p. 43, by permission of the publisher.

tory because it depends too heavily upon the exact positions of the extreme scores. A single score falling appreciably higher or lower than the remainder of the scores will affect the range disproportionately.

A more satisfactory measure of variability is the *quartile deviation,* or semi-interquartile range. The first quartile in a distribution, Q_1, is the point below which one fourth of the measures lie. The third quartile, Q_3, is the point below which three fourths of the measures lie. (The second quartile, Q_2, is the same as the median.) The quartiles are located by counting and interpolation. The quartile deviation, Q, is equal to half the difference between Q_3 and Q_1. In other words,

$$Q = \frac{Q_3 - Q_1}{2}.$$

If the distribution is asymmetrical, $Md + Q$ may not equal Q_3 and $Md - Q$ may not equal Q_1, but the differences will probably be small. As a result $Md \pm Q$ will define the range of approximately the middle 50 per cent of the scores (see Fig. 4-2). For example, if Md is 60 and Q is 20, half of the scores lie between 40 and 80 while one fourth of them lie above 80 and the other fourth lie below 40. When the median is the measure of central tendency used, the quartile deviation is the most appropriate measure of variability. These two measures are suitable for use with small samples where great accuracy is neither implied nor possible.

The most important and universally accepted measure of variability is the *standard deviation,* indicated by σ (lower-case sigma). The standard deviation is the root-mean-square of the deviations from the mean. In other words, it is the square root of the mean of the squared deviations from the mean of the distribution. It is computed by the formula

$$\sigma = \sqrt{\frac{\Sigma x^2}{N}},$$

where x is the difference between the individual score and the group mean.

The standard deviation, like the quartile deviation, provides a basis for judging how good a score is relative to a normal distribution. The range defined by $M \pm \sigma$ includes approximately 68 per cent of the scores in a normal distribution; 34 per cent of these are above the mean and 34 per cent are below. The range defined by $M \pm 2\sigma$ includes approximately 95 per cent of the cases, equally divided above and below the mean, and the range defined by $M \pm 3\sigma$ include approximately 99.7 per cent of the cases (see Fig. 4-1). Thus, if M is 60 and σ is 18, we know that some 68 per cent of the scores lie between 42 and 78 and that a student with a score of 96 is surpassed by only some 2 per cent of his classmates. Estimates of this sort may be made throughout the entire distribution with the aid of a standard statistical table.[1]

The standard deviation is the most stable, dependable, and widely used measure of variability. Mathematically, it is compatible with most other measures, including the mean, and it serves as the basis for several other statistics. It should be the measure of variability used in serious research studies, especially when other statistics are subsequently to be computed.

RELATIVE POSITION

The simplest measure of relative position is *rank*. Rank is obtained by counting down in order from the highest score to the score in question. To say that a score has a rank of 20 means that only 19 are better. Rank scores are difficult to interpret. A rank of 20 would carry quite a different connotation if there were 220 in the group than if there were only 22.

The use of *percentile rank* represents an attempt to overcome the difficulty of interpreting rank scores. A percentile score is stated in terms of the percentage of scores a given score equals or exceeds. A percentile rank of 90, for example, means that the score in question equals or exceeds 90 per cent of the scores in the group.

The *standard score* is a particularly useful measure in comparing scores from dissimilar tests. A standard score (z-score) is expressed in units of standard deviation above or below the mean. This score, like the percentile rank, can indicate the positions of individuals on different tests, where raw scores are usually of no help. A standard score of $+1.75$ means that the individual scored 1.75 sigmas above the mean of the group. From the table cited one may find that such a score is exceeded by only four students out of 100. A standard score of $-.90$ means that the student scored .90 sigma below the mean of the group, a position surpassed by 82 students out of 100. The standard score makes it possible to interpret scores readily without knowing how many students there were in the group, how many items there were on the test, or what the mean and standard deviation were.

[1] Available, for example, in 20:446.

The term "standard score" also has a generic meaning. It may refer to various other special techniques for expressing a score based on the mean and standard deviation of the group, such as the T-score, which is based on a mean of 50 and a σ of 10, and the stanine score, which is based on a mean of 5 and a σ of 2.

RELATIONSHIP

Suppose that in comparing the results of tests in music and English the elementary teacher notices that the student who received the highest score in music also received the highest score in English, the student who received the second highest score in music also received the second highest score in English, and so forth throughout the distribution. The relative positions of the pupils on the two tests correspond perfectly and indicate a high degree of association, or *correlation*, between the tests. In this instance the relationship is said to be a perfect positive correlation, represented by a correlation coefficient of 1.00.

Suppose, on the other hand, that the student who made the highest score on the music test made the lowest score on the English test and that the relative positions of the students on the two tests were exactly reversed. Such a relationship is known as a perfect negative correlation and would be represented by a correlation coefficient of -1.00. Very seldom are distributions related in such clear-cut fashion. If the relationship between the two tests were strictly a random one, the correlation coefficient would be .00.

Correlation is a measure of the degree of association between two variables. There are several methods for computing correlation, but the most widely accepted is the Pearson product-moment method, expressed by the formula

$$r = \frac{\Sigma xy}{N\sigma_x\sigma_y},$$

where r is the coefficient of correlation, xy is the product of the deviation of an X score from the group mean and the deviation of a Y score from the group mean, N is the number of pairs of scores, σ_x is the standard deviation of the X scores, and σ_y is the standard deviation of the Y scores.

When data are expressed as ranks rather than as scores or when the sampling is small, the Spearman rank-difference method may be adequate. It is expressed by the formula

$$\rho = 1 - \frac{6\Sigma D^2}{N(N^2-1)},$$

where ρ (rho) is the coefficient of correlation, N is the number of pairs of scores, and D is the difference between the individual's rank on two tests.

It is important to remember that a coefficient of correlation is merely an indication of the degree of association between two variables and does not imply the presence or direction of a cause-and-effect relationship. One may know that A and B tend to vary together, but he does not necessarily know whether A depends upon B, whether B depends upon A, whether both depend upon an unknown, C, or whether they vary together entirely by chance. Interpreting the nature of the relationship is a matter of logic rather than statistics.

The practice of referring to coefficients of correlation as either high or low is sometimes misleading. High and low are relative terms. An r of .40 would be low if one were correlating two music aptitude batteries, but it would be high if one were correlating music aptitude scores with the height of the individuals. A correlation coefficient must be judged in the light of the nature of the variables being correlated and in the light of similar results for the same variables reported by other observers.

The technique of analyzing the correlations between groups of tests to determine what elements they have in common is known as *factor analysis*. Most tests of special abilities overlap in content, and, by careful study of the extent of this overlapping, psychologists can sometimes isolate and identify elemental factors comprising the abilities. The task is complex and requires training (3, 11, 23, 35, 67).

STATISTICAL RELIABILITY

Statistical data are ordinarily obtained from a small random sampling of the population.[2] Often, we cannot collect data from the entire group with which we are concerned. Consequently, the true value we seek can never be determined with perfect accuracy. The best we can do is to estimate the value on the basis of the data we have. In addition, however, we can estimate how close we have probably come to the true value.

If we obtain several different samplings from the same population, we will find that they do not yield identical results, although the differences are usually small. There exists a distribution of sample values which cluster around the true value according to the normal probability curve. The mean and the standard deviation of this sampling distribution may be easily computed. The standard deviation of the sampling distribution is known as the *standard error*. Standard error indicates the amount of variability in a statistic rather than in a group of scores or individuals. Of course, it is only the obtained values that vary; the true value does not. Because the distribution of sample values takes the form of a normal probability curve, we know that for each 100 individuals with a given true score 68 will have obtained scores within 1 standard error (S.E.) of the true score, 95 will have obtained scores within 2 S.E. of the true score, and so forth. Though a statistician would avoid such a statement on technical grounds, for practical purposes the teacher can say that the chances are 68 out of 100 that a student's true score lies within 1 S.E. of his obtained score and 95 out of 100 that it lies within 2 S.E. of his obtained score. The standard error is normally attached to the obtained value by a plus-or-

---

[2] "Population" refers to the entire group under observation.

minus sign. Thus, if one encounters the figure 75 ± 1.5, he may conclude that the chances are 95 out of 100 that the true value lies between 72 and 78.

Standard error formulas have been computed for use with a number of statistics:

1. *Standard Error of Measurement* (Standard Error of an Obtained Score)

$$S.E._{\text{meas}} = \sigma\sqrt{1-r},$$

where σ is the standard deviation and r is the reliability coefficient of the test.

2. *Standard Error of the Mean*

$$S.E._M = \frac{\sigma}{\sqrt{N}}$$

3. *Standard Error of the Difference Between Two Means*

$$S.E._{A-B} = \sqrt{(S.E._A)^2 + (S.E._B)^2},$$

where A and B are the two means.

4. *Standard Error of the Pearson Coefficient of Correlation*

$$S.E._r = \frac{1-r^2}{\sqrt{N}}$$

Reliability r's are lower when computed by the split-half method because the effective length of the test is reduced. Similarly, validity r's are lower when a measure is compared with a criterion measure of only moderate reliability. Formulas are also available for correcting these and other coefficients of correlation to compensate for the imperfect reliabilities of the measures being compared.

Probable error (P.E.), another measure of reliability, is the quartile deviation of the sampling distribution. It is derived from the standard deviation and is reported in the same form as standard error. An author must indicate when the error attached to a measure is probable error; otherwise, the reader will take it to be standard error. Because $Md \pm 3Q$ defines the range of the middle 96 per cent of the cases, if a measure is reported as 82.6 ± 1.8, using probable error, one may say, for example, that the chances are 96 out of 100 that the true value of the measure lies between 77.2 and 88.0.

LEVELS
OF SIGNIFICANCE

In comparing two measures one can never be absolutely certain that the obtained difference reflects a genuine difference. It may be that one or both of the measures have been unduly affected by chance variations in sampling and that the same procedures if performed with a different sampling would yield a different result. The probability that the obtained result is not due to chance is known as *significance*. Significance is normally reported in terms of a *level of significance,* or *level of confidence,* which represents the probability that the obtained result is due to chance and that no true difference exists. If a measure is reported to be significant at the .05 (or 5 per cent) level, the chances are no more than 5 out of 100 that the result is attributable to chance. For example, if a difference between two means is reported to be significant at the .05 level, the chances are at least 95 out of 100 that a true difference exists. The significance of a difference between two means is often evaluated by means of a statistic known as *t,* which is the ratio of the difference between the means to the standard error of that difference.

The level of significance is always derived from the standard error of the measure. The usual practice is to report significance at either the .05 level or the .01 level. Probabilities above .05 are normally considered not significant. If an obtained result is found to be significant at only the .10 level, for example, the chances are 10 out of 100 that it is due to chance factors, and decisions based on such findings may prove incorrect as often as once in 10 times. For most statistical purposes this would be considered inadequate, though the level at which findings are meaningful depends entirely upon the use to which they are to be put. Suppose that an experiment with a new teaching technique produces better results but the findings are significant at only the .15 level. If the technique requires no additional expenditure of time, money, or effort, and if its failure would produce no harmful effects, it might be worth trying on a broader basis. On the other hand, if basic curriculum changes are involved, most administrators would want greater assurance that the experimental results were not due to chance.

The researcher may set an arbitrary level in advance above which he will consider his findings significant and below which he will consider them not significant. However, it is much better to report the level at which the findings are significant and leave the decision as to whether or not that level is adequate to the individual reader, who may contemplate using the findings in another context. In this way a portion of the responsibility for interpretation is shifted to the consumer, a practice now adopted by the U.S. Weather Bureau. Under what is known as probability forecasting, the Bureau will state, for example, that the probability of rain during the day is 60 per cent, and deciding whether or not to carry an umbrella is left to the individual.

THE NULL HYPOTHESIS

Many of the research studies in music education today involve a comparison between two groups, frequently an experimental group and a control group. Such studies often hinge upon whether or not there exists a genuine difference between the groups in the characteristic being evaluated. The usual procedure is to assume that no real difference exists and then test the assumption to find the level of significance at which it may be accepted or rejected. The assumption that no real difference exists is known as the *null hypothesis*. If it is shown, for example, that the null hypothesis may be rejected at the .01 level in a given experiment, this means that the chances are 99 out of 100 that a true difference exists. In any action taken on the basis of such findings, we are likely to be right 99 times out of 100 and wrong only once.

The use of the null hypothesis places the experimenter in a much more sound position logically than he would otherwise be. Instead of using his evidence in attempting to prove a positive hypothesis, he uses it in attempting to disprove or discredit the null hypothesis. The null hypothesis is analogous to the legal principle that a person is innocent until proven guilty. If the obtained difference is too large to be attributable to chance, the experimenter rejects the null hypothesis and accepts the alternate hypothesis, namely, that a true difference exists. Normally, a level of significance of .01 or .05 is considered adequate to reject the null hypothesis without assuming undue risk but if the null hypothesis is found to be true, the investigator cannot reject it and must conclude that there is indeed no genuine difference.

Statistical method, like other techniques of research, is based on logical thought on the part of the investigator. No research technique can produce dependable and meaningful results if it is used or interpreted incorrectly. Every music educator who plans to undertake research of his own should be certain not only that he is familiar with the statistical tools available to him but that he also understands the logic upon which they are based.

5

Teacher-Made Tests

The appropriateness of a test to accomplish the aims of the teacher should be the most important criterion in test selection. If a standardized test or other published test is available that fills the teacher's need, he should consider using it, but it is a great mistake to assume that all published tests are standardized or that all published tests are good. If there is no suitable test available, he must prepare one himself. A test written by a teacher for a specific purpose is sometimes preferable to a standardized test. Many instrumental teachers have designed their own informal measures of musical aptitude.

The advantages of a teacher-made test over a standardized test include the following:

1. A teacher-made test can be adapted to fit the specific needs and objectives of a given teacher, school, or situation.

2. In some subject-matter fields there are no suitable standardized tests. It is usually better for a teacher to write his own test having face validity than to use a standardized test of questionable validity.

3. Teacher-made tests cost less to administer than standardized tests.

4. Standardized tests, of necessity, are composed of objective items. They do not include essay questions, and this omission deprives the teacher of a useful tool for evaluating certain types of learning.

5. Teacher-made tests do not require the advanced planning that standardized tests require, although it is debatable whether this is an advantage or a disadvantage.

Standardized tests, on the other hand, possess certain advantages, including the following:

1. Most standardized tests have been revised several times and have been strengthened in the process. Weak and nondiscriminating items have been removed.

2. Because of the revision that they have undergone, standardized tests tend to be more reliable than teacher-made tests.

3. Standardized tests are usually constructed by experts in the subject-matter field, often in collaboration with experts in testing. They are likely to be technically superior to teacher-made tests.

4. Standardized tests are accompanied by norms showing the mean scores obtained by large numbers of students, classified by age, training, sex, or other criteria; thus, the teacher can compare the performance of his students with the performance of similar students on a national basis.

5. Standardized tests save time in preparation. They may also save time in scoring, particularly if they are machine scored.

PRINCIPLES OF
TEST CONSTRUCTION

1. The most important task of the teacher when he undertakes to construct a test is to define clearly in his own mind the objectives of his test. One should never test without having a definite aim.

2. It is extremely important that the test content comprise a balanced, representative sampling of the course content. This criterion, essential for validity, is normally satisfied in teacher-made tests by inspection.

3. To a greater or lesser extent, testing should emphasize not merely the mechanical recall of facts but also the application of knowledge. If education is to be meaningful, it must be applied in the day-to-day situations one faces in life.

4. In every test item the teacher must be certain that his answer is the correct one. This maxim appears so patently obvious that it scarcely need be mentioned, yet it is often violated. In dealing with a subject that is controversial or inadequately understood by scholars, the teacher should be certain that his information is the most authoritative and up-to-date information available and that experts would agree on the answer. This holds true in teaching as well as in evaluation, but it is especially unfair in an examination to expect an answer that represents nothing more than the personal opinion of the examiner. If there is any doubt, an authority should be cited in the test item: "According to Grout, ..."

5. Specific test items that are used repeatedly should be subjected to *item analysis*. Item analysis refers to the evaluation of the effectiveness of individual test items by means of such statistics as the *difficulty value* and the *discrimination value*. The difficulty value is the percentage of persons

who answer a given item correctly. Items with difficulty values of 40 to 60 are considered moderately difficult. An item with a difficulty value of 90 is easy, and an item with a value of 10 is difficult. An examination should include items representing a reasonably wide range of difficulty values, but there should not be an excessive number of extremely difficult or extremely easy items. The discrimination value of an item is a measure of the extent to which persons who answer the item correctly tend to score high on the test. It may be derived by correlating the test scores with whether or not the individuals answered the item correctly. The usual practice is to compare only the highest and lowest thirds or fourths of the test papers. If the students who earn the highest scores tend to miss a particular item appreciably more than do the students who earn the lowest scores, there is very likely something wrong with the item.

6. Each of the various kinds of test items, e.g., true-false, multiple-choice, is particularly suited to specific types of information. The instructor should always select the kind of test item that appears most appropriate to the type of learning he is seeking to evaluate. For example, essay questions would probably be less suitable than multiple-choice items if one is testing on the elements of musical notation.

7. Optional questions should be included on examinations only when there is a specific reason for doing so. The generous use of optional questions in order to permit a student to by-pass items for which he is poorly prepared is questionable.

8. The test should be constructed so that the effects of such extraneous factors as reading rate and comprehension are minimized. The writer should make it as easy as possible for the student to respond.

9. The teacher constructing a test should review the discussion in Chapter 3 of reliability, validity, objectivity, ease of administration, proper organization, and other criteria of a good test.

The test should be scored immediately, the papers handed back to the students, and the results discussed with them. This practice can be an effective instructional technique because every student is directly involved with every test item. The student is likely to remember the material longer if he has gone over it in this manner than if he has not.

ORAL TESTS

From ancient times, through the rise of the medieval universities, to modern times, oral examinations were more common than written ones. They are easier for the examiner to compose than are written examinations, although they still must be prepared and cannot be entirely improvised. They allow far more flexibility in identifying the particular strengths and weaknesses of the individual, and they allow the examiner to give cues when necessary. The principal reason that oral testing has largely been superseded by written techniques is that the teacher simply does not have the time to evaluate each student adequately by oral methods.

Oral testing is more commonly used in teaching situations than in evaluative situations. The teacher asks a question of the class or of an individual in the class and uses the response as a point of departure for classroom teaching. Oral testing may also serve as a supplement to written testing, though it seldom serves as a substitute at the elementary or secondary levels.

Oral testing is important in American education at the graduate level, where candidates for the masters degree and the doctorate are usually examined orally. During the course of an oral examination, the ability of the student to verbalize becomes as apparent as his knowledge of the subject matter, though, unhappily, the two are not always related. For this reason it is difficult to grade an oral examination objectively, and it is difficult to make comparative evaluations of students on the basis of oral examinations. It is easier for the examiner to be influenced by such factors as the student's vocabulary, mannerisms, and personality in an oral examination than in a written one. The instructor must constantly be alert to distinguish those factors that are pertinent to the examination from those that are not.

TRUE-FALSE ITEMS

True-false items are among the easiest to score, but they are perhaps the most troublesome of all items to write. The basic limitation of true-false tests lies in the difficulty of constructing statements that are not ambiguous or equivocal. Ambiguity often passes unnoticed by the teacher, who views each item in the context in which he wrote it; but a test item defective in this respect can appear extremely complicated to the bright student, who may discover in the statement implications that had not occurred to the teacher. Even if the student guesses correctly what was in the mind of the test author, he is placed in a disadvantageous position relative to the average or poor student merely by having to spend the time it takes to consider the matter.

The true-false test is often criticized as being highly susceptible to guessing. There are only two responses possible, and if a student makes a random guess for each item or if he answers all the items with the same response, he should score approximately 50 per cent. It is a simple matter for the teacher to discount the effects of guessing by subtracting the number of wrong answers from the number of correct answers. Because only two responses are possible, the teacher may assume that the student missed half of the items on which he guessed. For each item he missed by guessing, there was an item he answered correctly by guessing. Therefore, by knowing the number of items missed, the instructor can deduct the number of correct answers that were achieved by guessing. The class should be notified in advance when this "rights-minus-wrongs" formula is to be applied. Under these conditions if a student is uncertain of an answer, he should leave the item blank. If no response is made, the item will not be counted correct, of course, but neither will it offset one of the correct answers. Some teachers always prefer to have their students guess when they are uncertain of answers. They claim that real-life situations require guessing and that the ability to make an educated guess, even on the basis of inadequate background information, is necessary and should be developed. Unless instructed otherwise, the student will probably assume that he should guess if he is uncertain.

The true-false item is difficult to use in testing the application of basic principles to new situations, and its popularity has diminished considerably since the period following World War I. Nevertheless, well-written true-false tests provide a simple and direct means of measuring factual recall and can play an important role in the testing program.

In writing true-false items the instructor should consider the following principles:

1. If a statement is partially true, that portion which is false should be prominent and important enough to justify marking the entire statement false. Trivialities ought not to make a statement false, e.g., "The Music Educators National Conference was founded in 1907." The fact that the organization was not known by precisely that name in 1907 ought not to make the item false. However, it is not a good test item because the knowledgeable student might reason in just that manner. A better version would be: "The organization now known as the Music Educators National Conference was founded in 1907."

2. Statements that require qualitative judgments should be avoided. An item such as "The music of Meyerbeer is more lyrical than that of Spohr" is arbitrary and unsupportable. Quantitative terms should be used when possible. "Beethoven wrote nine symphonies" is preferable to "Beethoven wrote several symphonies." However, it is still worthless as a test item; it might be marked false by the student who is aware of the "Battle Symphony."

3. Items that depend upon logic or interpretation should be avoided unless it is the ability to reason or interpret that is being tested. "Haydn wrote nine symphonies" would be a confusing true-false statement. Of course, he wrote many more than nine, but one cannot deny that he did, in fact, write nine symphonies.

4. True-false items should not be excessively long and involved, and they should not require numerous qualifying phrases. Very lengthy items are probably true more often than not, though there may be some teachers whose longer items tend to be false.

5. Statements should be positive rather than negative because negative statements can be confusing to the reader, e.g., "It is not true that the sonatina lacks a development section."

6. Specific words, phrases, and other determiners that give a clue to the answer should be avoided. For example, true-false statements containing the words "never" or "always" are usually false. On the other hand, such phrases as "generally speaking" often suggest that the writer is trying to construct a true statement. Vague and imprecise terms should not be used.

7. The teacher should be certain that the correct responses comprise a random mixture of true and false and that there is no pattern discernible, such as two trues and one false. Also, the teacher should be certain that there is a reasonable numerical balance between the true and false items.

The letters "T" and "F" are not entirely satisfactory as responses on true-false tests because when hastily written they can look remarkably similar. The use of + and ○ represents a distinct improvement, for these symbols are clearly dissimilar. An alternative procedure is to include the words "true" and "false" or the letters "T" and "F" before each item and let the student circle the correct word or letter.

As a modification of the usual true-false test, some teachers ask their students to revise each false statement to make it true. Often there is more than one way in which a statement can be revised, and some ways may demonstrate greater insight than others. The teacher may underline a word or phrase in each item and have the student modify the underlined phrases in the false statements in order to make the statements true.

MULTIPLE-CHOICE ITEMS

Multiple-choice items are probably the most widely used and most highly regarded type of objective test items. A multiple-choice item is less susceptible to guessing than a true-false item, it provides its own frame of reference for judging the appropriateness of each response, and it may be applied to many types of learning. Nevertheless, critics complain that even the multiple-choice item is often ambiguous, superficial, and excessively vulnerable to guessing.

The teacher preparing multiple-choice items should keep in mind the following principles:

1. Each item should be based on a meaningful, demonstrably valid statement concerning an important idea. There should be no doubt that experts would agree on the answer.

2. Each response should be plausible. If two or three of the choices are so farfetched that they are obviously incorrect, the discriminating power of the item is reduced accordingly. The incorrect responses should be framed in such a way that they appear credible to the student who has a superficial knowledge of the topic and thus distinguish him from the student who has a thorough knowledge.

3. All responses should be as brief as possible, and the correct response should be approximately equal to the others in length. Students often tend to choose a response that is noticeably longer or shorter than the others.

4. Each of the choices must be correct grammatically. That is, the opening portion, which is known as the *stem*, must form a grammatically correct and meaningful statement when read with each of the possible responses. For example, if the stem ends with the article "an" while each of the responses except one requires "a," it is obvious which response is correct. This difficulty can be avoided by including the article with each response rather than with the stem.

5. Negative or ambiguous statements should be avoided, and any consistent pattern of correct responses should also be avoided.

6. In the directions it is usually wise to ask the student to indicate the "best" answer rather than the "correct" answer, e.g., "Place the number identifying the best response in the blank preceding the number of each item." However, even the use of "best" does not relieve the test writer of

his responsibility to construct good test items. If there can be argument about the answer, the writer has not done his job well. "They're all correct, but I like this one best" is an indefensible position.

Inserting "none of these" or "all of these" among the possible responses is a useful device to reduce the effects of guessing and to make the item somewhat more difficult. The use of the former requires that the student decide not only among the choices listed but among the many choices not listed. Including this alternative makes it necessary for the teacher to examine the item very carefully to make certain that there is not a better answer than the one he thought of.

The number of alternative responses in multiple-choice tests is usually four or five. It is sometimes difficult to remember more than five choices as one reads a question. If a teacher wishes to compensate for the effects of guessing, he should subtract from the total correct one third of the incorrect responses in a four-choice test or one fourth of the incorrect responses in a five-choice test. The formula is

$$S = R - \frac{W}{N-1} \, ,$$

where S is the corrected score, R is the number right, W is the number wrong, and N is the number of possible responses.

MATCHING ITEMS

Matching exercises consist of a column of statements or phrases, each preceded by parentheses or a blank, and a parallel column of responses, each identified by a letter or number. The directions usually ask the student to place in the blank preceding each statement in Column 1 the letter identifying the response in Column 2 which best completes (or is most closely associated with) the statement.

The matching examination is particularly useful in testing concise matters of factual recall that involve pairing or association, such as keys and their signatures, composers of specific works, or birth dates of composers. The following principles should be kept in mind in constructing matching examinations:

1. The most important principle is that only homogeneous statements and responses should be included in each group. In other words, Column 2 may include either names, dates, places, compositions, or other lists of like information, but different types of information must not be mixed in the same list. If they are, the student's chances of guessing the correct answer are greatly increased. For example, if it is clear that the answer is a date and there are only two dates among the responses, the chances are at least one out of two that the student will guess correctly. Matching examinations should be broken down so that the various kinds of information are included in separate lists.

2. Matching groups should include approximately six to fifteen items and should include a few more responses than are needed. If a response may be used more than once, the student should be so informed.

3. Each matching group should be contained on a single page. The student should not be required to look back and forth from one page to another. The responses should be listed in random order.

4. After he has prepared a group of matching items, the instructor must carefully check each response against each statement to make certain that no "incorrect" response is as satisfactory as his intended response.

COMPLETION ITEMS

In a completion item the student is to supply the missing word or phrase in an incomplete statement or definition. It is especially difficult to construct completion items that are neither ambiguous nor obvious. The following principles apply:

1. Only important words should be omitted, and there should be enough information remaining to make the statement recognizable. Normally, there should be no more than two omissions in each sentence.

2. There must be no grammatical or syntactical clues that might reveal the answer. For example, the form of the article ("a" or "an"), the number of the pronoun or verb (singular or plural), and similar clues sometimes greatly simplify the choice the student must make.

3. Blanks should be of uniform length and should not reflect the length of the correct responses.

4. It is easier to score completion items if the responses are written in blanks provided along the left or right margins than if they are inserted at the proper places in the sentences.

5. The instructor should grant some credit for every acceptable response. The better the item is written, the fewer responses will be acceptable.

ESSAY TESTS

Although the essay test is less suitable than objective tests for the measurement of specific facts, it is the most appropriate type of test for measuring understanding and attitude. It can provide insight into the creative potential of the student and indicate the extent of his originality. The broad scope of expression it makes possible is unmatched by other types of tests. It emphasizes Gestalt concepts of wholeness.

Essay questions are somewhat easier to construct than objective items; however, because so few questions may be used, each must be carefully thought out and precisely worded. The student should be told clearly and unequivocally what he is expected to do. The questions should be distributed or written on the chalkboard by the teacher and not merely read to the students.

The value of essay tests depends to a considerable extent upon the uniformity with which they are scored. It is important that the instructor identify clearly the answers he is seeking at the time he writes the questions. Such a procedure not only provides valuable guidelines when the time comes to score the tests; it also helps to insure that each question will accomplish the purposes it was designed to accomplish.

Essay questions cannot be scored with absolute objectivity. Reliability in essay testing refers not only to the reliability of the test but also to the reliability of the scoring. Experiments have shown that distressing discrepancies sometimes occur when different teachers are asked to score the same set of essay examinations or even when a teacher is asked to score the same set twice.

The teacher should read the examination papers question by question rather than student by student. That is, he should read each answer to the first question, assign each a numerical score or other evaluation, read each answer to the second question, and so forth. By totaling the scores for the individual questions, he has a more solid basis for comparison among the papers than if he reads each student's paper separately, in which case he may find that at the end he is not evaluating by the selfsame standards used at the beginning. This inconsistency, which may be due to fatigue or to forgetting, is particularly dangerous if the papers are not read at one sitting. As an alternative some instructors prefer to give each paper a preliminary reading and place it in one of five piles corresponding to the usual letter grades. Those that are considered borderline cases may be so indicated. Then the instructor will go over the papers again to verify his earlier evaluations, paying particular attention to the borderline cases.

One important source of inconsistency associated with the scoring of essay examinations is the phenomenon known as the *halo effect*. The term refers to the tendency to evaluate the paper of a student known to be a good student higher than is deserved on the basis of the answers he has written. Conversely, the paper of a poor student may be rated lower than is justified on the basis of his answers. This is not to imply that the instructor is at all dishonest but merely that he is unconsciously influenced by past experience. The halo effect may also cause some answers to be rated higher than they might otherwise be when other answers on the same paper are particularly good. Identifying the papers by numbers rather than by names and reading the answers question by question are the most effective means of eliminating the halo effect.

Although the essay examination is less susceptible to guessing and cheating than the objective examination, it is considerably more susceptible to bluffing. A skillful writer can prepare an impressive essay answer that uses the appropriate vocabulary and appears to show broad background but upon closer examination says nothing. This is a technique that is well developed by some students. The instructor must decide when he writes the question what he expects in the answer, and he must score on that basis regardless of how much padding the answer contains.

6

Tests of
Musical Aptitude

Since the early days of the testing movement, a large portion of the efforts of test writers in music has been directed toward the measurements of aptitude for musical study. An analysis of these tests reveals clearly the content, procedures, and psychological bases that have characterized music aptitude testing in the United States and Great Britain. The tests discussed in this book are the tests known to be available commercially as of September, 1967. They are listed chronologically in order of their first appearance, with the following information: author, dates of publication (or copyright) and revision, publisher, address of publisher, grade or age levels, forms available, cost, and time required. Out-of-print tests are listed in the appendix.

SEASHORE MEASURES
OF MUSICAL TALENTS*

The 1919 version of the battery, by Seashore alone, contained five recorded tests, entitled Sense of Pitch,

* Carl E. Seashore, Don Lewis, and Joseph G. Saetveit. 1919, 1939, 1956, 1960. The Psychological Corporation, 304 E. 45th St., New York, N. Y. 10017. Grades 4-16 and adult. Series A. $12 per set, including manual, 33⅓ rpm recording, scoring stencils, and 50 machine-scorable answer sheets. 60 minutes.

Intensity Discrimination, Sense of Time, Sense of Consonance, and Tonal Memory. A sixth test, Sense of Rhythm, was added six years later. The battery was completely revised in 1939, at which time a test of timbre was substituted for the consonance test. The subsequent revisions have dealt with minor technical matters. The six tests, now redesignated simply Pitch, Loudness, Rhythm, Time, Timbre, and Tonal Memory, are available on a single 33⅓ rpm recording. The recording is excellent, but the voice of the announcer is excessively deliberate and constitutes a distraction for some groups.

Series A, designed for unselected groups, is now the only form available. Series B, a more difficult version for selected groups, appeared in 1939 but was discontinued in 1947. Series C, for refined laboratory work with individuals, was projected but never published. The answer sheets may be scored by machine or by hand. Each sheet should be inspected before scoring to be certain that the student has made only one response for each item. It is advisable on this and other tests of comparable length to examine young children in two or more sessions.

The pitch test originally contained 100 pairs of tones produced by tuning forks. The examinee, or subject, was required to judge whether the second tone of each pair was higher or lower in pitch than the first. The variations ranged from 30 cycles per second (cps) to ½ cps, or approximately from 120 cents to 2 cents.[1] The 1939 version contains only 50 items, though the test can be repeated to raise the reliability slightly. The procedure is the same. The tones of the pitch test, as well as those of the loudness, rhythm, and time tests, are produced by a beat-frequency oscillator. The standard tone has a frequency of 500 cps. There are five pairs with a difference of 17 cps, seven with a difference of 12 cps, 10 of 8 cps, 10 of 5 cps, eight of 4 cps, five of 3 cps, and five of 2 cps.[2] These differences correspond to differences ranging approximately from 59 cents to 9 cents.

The intensity discrimination test was redesignated the loudness test, in accordance with the subtle but fundamental distinction between the physical characteristics of tone and their psychological manifestations. The loudness test contains 50 pairs of pure tones of 440 cps, and the subject is asked to judge whether the second tone is stronger or weaker than the first. There are five pairs with a difference of 4.0 decibels (db), five with a difference of 2.5 db, and 10 pairs each with differences of 2.0, 1.5, 1.0, and 0.5 db.

The rhythm test contains 30 pairs of rhythmic patterns. The subject is asked to judge whether the second pattern is the same as or different from the first. Short pulses of pure tone were substituted in the 1939 revision for the clicks of the original version. The frequency of the pulses is 500 cps. The test comprises 10 pairs of five-note patterns in 2-4 meter, 10 pairs of six-note patterns in 3-4 meter, and 10 pairs of seven-note patterns in 4-4 meter.

The test of time consists of 50 pairs of tones. The subject is instructed

---

[1] A cent is 1/100 of a semitone.
[2] Most of the technical data cited are from the respective test manuals.

to judge whether the second tone of each pair is longer or shorter than the first. The frequency of the tones is 440 cps, and the length of the standard tone is .8 sec. There are five pairs in which the difference is .30 sec., five pairs with a difference of .20 sec., 10 pairs each with differences of .15, .125, and .10 sec., and five pairs each with differences of .075 and .05 sec. In the original version of the time test, the subject heard three clicks and was asked to tell whether the second interval of time was longer or shorter than the first. The substitution of "filled" time for "empty" time was regarded by some critics as an important improvement.

In the timbre test, consisting of 50 pairs of tones, the subject is asked to judge whether the two tones of each pair are the same or different in timbre, or tone quality. Each tone consists of six partials with a fundamental frequency of 180 cps. The intensities of the partials of the standard tone, expressed in relation to the strongest, are -8, -6, 0, -11, -12, and -14.5 db. The variations in timbre are produced by reciprocal alterations in the intensities of the third and fourth partials. Alterations, where made, are as follows:

Item Numbers	db Increase in 4th Partial	db Decrease in 3rd Partial
1-10	10.0	9.6
11-20	8.5	4.0
21-30	7.0	2.4
31-40	5.5	1.2
41-50	4.0	0.7

The reliability of any recorded test depends to a certain extent upon the quality of the playback equipment used and upon the acoustical properties of the room, but the timbre test is especially vulnerable in this respect.

The tonal memory test contains 30 pairs of tonal sequences, including 10 pairs of three notes each, 10 pairs of four notes, and 10 pairs of five notes. One note of each pair is different in the two presentations, and the subject is required to identify by number the note that is different. The original version also included 10 pairs of two-note sequences and 10 pairs of six-note sequences. The sequences are played on an electronic organ. The smallest difference included is one step, though semitone differences were included in the original version.

The test of consonance originally included was widely criticized and was generally regarded to be the poorest test of the battery. The test contained 50 pairs of two-note chords, and the subject was instructed to indicate which chord of each pair was the more consonant in terms of blend, smoothness, and fusion. It soon became apparent that a number of extraneous factors were tending to influence the results. Though the test was dropped in 1939 as unworkable, Seashore still professed faith in the principle of testing the sense of consonance.

Reliability

The authors of the 1939 revision report the following reliabilities in the test manual:

Test	Grades 4-5	Grades 6-8	Grades 9-16
Pitch	.82	.84	.84
Loudness	.85	.82	.74
Rhythm	.67	.69	.64
Time	.72	.63	.71
Timbre	.55	.63	.68
Tonal Memory	.81	.84	.83

A number of investigators have reported reliabilities for at least some of the tests, often with astonishingly dissimilar results (4, 12, 15, 28, 41, 47, 57). Nearly all of the reliability and validity studies have been based on the 1919 version, which tended to be less reliable than the 1939 revision. The tests of pitch and tonal memory are usually found to be the most reliable tests of the Seashore battery, as well as other aptitude batteries. To many observers, they also have higher face validity.

Validity

Validity studies have been reported by numerous investigators (4, 12, 22, 28, 38, 39, 41, 60).[3] Teachers' ratings or grades in music courses have normally been used as the validating criteria. The results have varied widely and have included negative coefficients.

The controversy surrounding the basis for validating the Seashore tests has centered around two widely divergent schools of thought. Mursell, the principal spokesman for one of the schools, declared that the only way to determine whether the Seashore tests actually measured musical talent was to find out whether the persons who scored high and low on the tests also scored high and low in what Mursell called musical behavior, i.e., sight singing, playing the piano, passing courses in music theory, and so forth (43:16). This viewpoint, which is based on the assumed existence of a general factor of musicality, was referred to by Seashore as the *omnibus theory*. Seashore's own viewpoint, which he contrasted with the omnibus theory and referred to as the *theory of specifics*, denied the existence of a general factor of musical behavior and held that musicality is in fact a combination of a large number of separate and sometimes unrelated abilities. He argued that his tests must be validated only in terms of how successfully the factor being measured had been isolated. When the experimenter has measured in the laboratory the ability of the subject to discriminate between pitches and when all other factors have been controlled, Seashore maintained, no reasonable person could deny that the sense of pitch had indeed been measured. Further, he declared that it would be as absurd to validate the measurement against the judgment of even the finest musician or teacher as it would be to validate the reading on a thermometer against the judgment of a person sensitive to temperature. He rejected all attempts to validate his tests against external and

[3] For a summary of the findings of reliability and validity studies of the Seashore tests, see 42:292 and 42:296 or 33:204 and 33:208.

omnibus criteria, which he contended were less valid than the measures themselves (51:383–386). Mursell defended his position with equal vigor. Further, he questioned whether Seashore's specific abilities function in the same way when they are isolated as when they exist in a musical context.

Interpretation
of Results

One basic principle underlying the Seashore *Measures* is that the conclusion reached must be limited to the factor measured. Accordingly, Seashore warned, if a student scores in the 99th percentile on the pitch test, the examiner cannot conclude that the child is musical but can say only that he has an extraordinary sense of pitch. The student may be completely lacking in other basic talents or in such nonmusical requisites to success as motivation and self-discipline.

There can be no doubt that much of the criticism heaped upon the Seashore battery has been due to misinterpretation of the test results by untrained individuals who have concluded more than was justified on the basis of the scores. Seashore maintained that because the capacities measured by his battery are not the only components of musical talent, the *Measures* should be supplemented by intelligence scores, case histories, interviews, auditions, and other appropriate data. Further, he maintained that, although a high score on his battery may be accepted at face value, a low score requires verification to be certain that it is not due to misunderstanding of instructions, lack of motivation, illness, or other extrinsic factors.

Another principle underlying the Seashore battery is that the sensory capacities tend to be basic and elemental and for this reason exist in all humans regardless of training and experience. Seashore maintained that after a comparatively early age these capabilities do not vary in an individual, though their measurement may be inhibited by the young child's inability to understand the task and apply himself to it. If we measure these capacities in a child by the age of 10, the results are likely to remain more or less stable throughout his life, Seashore insisted, and in this way it is possible to identify musical talent before training is begun. He argued that aural acuity is analogous to visual acuity; just as no amount of training or maturation can increase the acuity of the eye, no amount of training or maturation can increase the acuity of the ear, though training and maturation can increase the ability of an individual to use both the eye and the ear (52:53).

According to Seashore the capacity of the sensory organs is subject to both a physiological limit and a cognitive limit. The physiological limit is largely dependent upon heredity and is relatively stable. Though it varies slightly due to organic changes resulting from maturation, such as the hardening of the ossicles of the middle ear, it establishes a limit beyond which training tends to be ineffective. The cognitive limit, on the other hand, results from environmental factors and lack of experience, which limit the ability of the individual to utilize his inherent capacity to the fullest. The cognitive limit can be raised with training and experience until it reaches the physiological limit.

The effects of training on the sensory capacities used in musical perception have been studied by several investigators. Many have reported no significant improvement or have attributed such improvement as does occur to changes in the testing situation, changes in the psychological outlook of the subject, and such (55, 58, 59, 47:40–41). Other experimenters, however, have demonstrated that appreciable improvement can be made with the proper kind of training (53, 71).

Most investigators who have studied the test intercorrelations have reported that they are low. These findings tend to confirm Seashore's position that the various capacities are relatively independent in the hierarchy of musical talent. It was this belief that caused Seashore to change the word "talent" in the title of the 1919 version to "talents" in the 1939 revision. Because of the independent nature of the capacities, Seashore insisted that it was meaningless to add the scores of the six tests and give a total score for the individual. Instead, he believed that the scores should be reported in the form of a *talent profile*, a graph showing each separate score and including other appropriate measures that may be available. The current Seashore answer sheet, which provides space for construction of a talent profile based on the six tests of the battery, may be seen in Fig. 6-1.

The profile technique was employed in the well-known Eastman experiment, in which Hazel Stanton tested the freshman classes of the Eastman School of Music from 1925 through 1928 and, on the basis of scores on the Seashore *Measures* and the *Iowa Comprehension Test*, an IQ test, classified each student in one of five groups with respect to his chances of graduation: safe, probable, possible, doubtful, or discouraged. She found that of the students in the safe group, 60 per cent were ultimately graduated, and that for the probable, possible, doubtful, and discouraged groups the respective percentages were 42, 33, 23, and 17 per cent (57). These results have been widely cited as evidence of the validity of the Seashore battery, but critics have pointed out that the issue is confused by the use of an IQ test. Perhaps the IQ test, supplemented by an audition, might serve just as well as the Seashore battery to predict success.

The major criticisms leveled against the Seashore battery, together with Seashore's replies, may be summarized as follows (51:305–6, 51:383–386):

1. The *Measures* are not valid.	1. The *Measures* have been validated internally for what they purport to measure. No omnibus validation is possible.
2. The *Measures* are not sufficiently reliable.	2. In a battery designed for "dragnet" testing, one cannot expect higher reliability. The upper half of the scores are sufficiently reliable for individual diagnosis; the lower half need re-investigation.

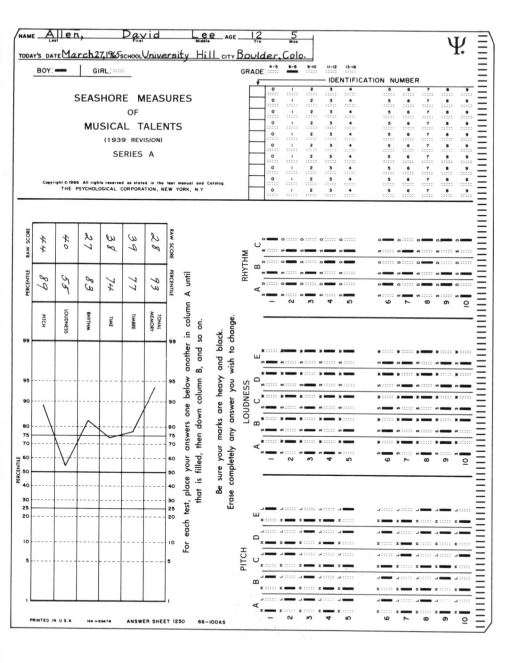

With a trained experimenter working under laboratory conditions, according to Seashore, all reliabilities are in the high 90's. Further, the reliability of a test can be improved by repeating it.

3. The *Measures* are atomistic. Genuine musical talent is more than the sum of a group of specific talents.

3. Seashore admitted the basic Gestalt nature of musical talent but maintained that any complex ability could best be studied by examining each aspect of it singly.

4. There are many factors important to musical success that are not measured by the battery.

4. Seashore acknowledged the truth of this contention but pointed out that there are few phenomena in the universe all aspects of which can be measured; in physics, for example, we must often rely on inductive reasoning. Furthermore, it is better to measure those factors that can be measured than to rely entirely on guessing.

5. Musical talent is largely a matter of training.

5. Seashore denied this and claimed that the overwhelming mass of evidence supported his denial.

6. The battery is not based upon musical materials. It is acoustical rather than musical.

6. Musical materials were deliberately avoided in order to escape the effects of musical training.

7. The same credit is given for answering the difficult items as for answering the easy ones.

7. The terms easy and difficult are relative. It is not practical to weight various items though the same effect may be achieved by including more difficult than easy items.

8. The *Measures* do not contain enough discriminating items. They are too easy. An adult scoring 27 on the rhythm test falls in the 55th percentile, while if he had answered only two more items correctly he would have scored in the 90th percentile.

8. If the *Measures* were more difficult, subjects would tend to become discouraged.

9. The tests are too long.

9. The 1939 revision is considerably shorter than the original version. Further shortening would jeopardize the reliability.

10. The battery discriminates against young subjects because of its length and its uninteresting nature.

10. This criticism is related to numbers six and nine. To adapt the battery to younger subjects, separate norms are provided for grades 4-5 and grades 6-8.

11. The number of each item should be announced on the recording. If a person becomes lost, he misses an entire section.

11. Announcing each item would substantially increase the time required to administer the battery. As an aid in keeping the place, the answer sheet is divided into columns of 10 answers each, and each column is announced on the recording.

The Seashore *Measures* have been used and tested extensively since their first appearance. For example, they have been administered in the public schools of Rochester, New York, continuously since 1930 to aid in assigning school-owned instruments, grouping students homogeneously, and choosing pupils for select performing groups (27). The battery has been subjected to all manner of experimentation. It has been modified for use with very young children (34), blind children (36), and other special groups. In addition to its many musical applications, it has been used in studies concerned with faulty speech, hearing, accent in foreign languages, and other fields of study (62, 10, 13). During World War I, the pitch and intensity tests were used to aid in the selection of candidates for training in submarine detection (47:47). There is an enormous body of literature dealing with the tests.

The Seashore battery is all the more remarkable when one considers that it was constructed completely without precedent. It has suffered through the years from popular and superficial advertising and publicity. Seashore well realized that his battery had limitations, and he stressed that it did not meet the popular demand for a simple, practical, and universal device for identifying musical talent. The problem is far too complex to permit such a simple solution. It now seems clear, however, that history will vindicate the battery as a useful tool when it is properly administered and when the results are properly interpreted.

KWALWASSER-DYKEMA MUSIC TESTS*

The Kwalwasser-Dykema, or K-D, battery consists of 10 tests: tonal memory, quality discrimination, intensity discrimination, tonal movement, time discrimination, rhythm discrimination, pitch discrimination, melodic taste, pitch imagery, and rhythm imagery. The test of tonal memory and the quality, intensity, time, rhythm, and pitch discrimination tests are similar in their psychological approach to the corresponding Seashore tests. The quality discrimination test employs instruments of the orchestra, however, and the pitch, time, and tonal memory tests require only that the subject indicate whether the pairs of tones or patterns are the same or different.

In the tonal movement test, the subject hears a series of four-note

* Jacob Kwalwasser and Peter W. Dykema. 1930. Carl Fischer, Inc., 62 Cooper Sq., New York, N. Y. 10003. Grades 4-16 and adult. $10.23 per set, including manual, 33⅓ rpm recording, scoring stencils, and 100 answer sheets. 60 minutes.

melodic patterns which are left unresolved; he must supply each cadence tone mentally and state whether it moves up or down from the last tone heard. The melodic taste test requires that the subject judge which of two brief melodies is better. In the pitch imagery and rhythm imagery tests, the subject must indicate whether the pattern played on the recording is the same as or different from the notation before him.

The manual contains norms for grades 4–6, 7–9, and 10–12, expressed as percentile ranks for each test and for the total. In other respects the manual is of very little help in interpreting the results. There is no information whatever on reliability and validity despite the long existence of the battery. Because of this inexcusable lack, the battery cannot claim to be adequately standardized. Those investigators who have studied the reliability and validity have obtained widely varying results and have reported a number of negative coefficients.[4] There is little question that both the reliability and the validity of the battery are inferior to Seashore's *Measures*. The reliability is so low that the battery is virtually useless for individual prognosis. Approximately 70 per cent of the individual test reliabilities reported have been below .50. Validated against grades and teacher ratings, very few coefficients above .40 have been reported. The technical quality of the recording is clearly inferior and constitutes a severe limitation of the K-D battery. The pitch discrimination test is especially unsatisfactory in this respect.

However, the K-D battery has several advantages over the Seashore *Measures:* (1) the individual tests are shorter, (2) the battery measures a wider variety of traits, (3) it is more interesting, (4) the stimuli are more musical, and (5) each item is announced on the recording. Unfortunately, these improvements appear to have been achieved at the expense of reliability. It makes little difference how easily one may gain information if the information is inaccurate.

The K-D answer sheet, like the Seashore answer sheet, provides a place for a talent profile. However, the K-D scores, unlike the Seashore scores, are added together to yield a composite total. The practice of totaling the scores of the individual tests may be questioned, even by advocates of the omnibus theory, unless the maximum score on each test is proportional to the relative importance of that trait as a component of musical talent and unless the means and standard deviations of the tests are comparable.

Critics have questioned whether the number of discriminating items contained in the various K-D tests is balanced. For example, a fifth grader who misses half of the items on the tonal movement test falls in the 48th percentile, but if he misses half of the items on the quality discrimination test, he falls in the 3rd percentile. Similarly, on the latter test, if he scores 21 out of the possible 30, he falls in the 59th percentile, but if he answers just one more item correctly, and his chances are 1 out of 2 of doing so on any one item, he immediately jumps to the 72nd percentile.

Because of its advantages the battery has enjoyed a certain popularity with music educators, but as more sophisticated batteries have become available, the limitations of the Kwalwasser-Dykema battery have become increasingly apparent.

[4] For a summary of the findings of these studies, see 33:212-213.

(WING) STANDARDISED
TESTS OF
MUSICAL INTELLIGENCE*

Also known as the *Wing Musical Aptitude Test*, this battery is now available on tape in English, German, French, and Swedish. All examples are played on the piano. An answer sheet for machine scoring may be obtained instead of the regular answer sheet. However, it contains no instructions, and the tape includes instructions for only the first three tests.

The first of the seven tests, chord analysis, consists of twenty tones or chords, and the subject is asked to check the number on the answer sheet corresponding to the number of pitches present. The answer sheet provides space for responses of up to six, but there are never more than four tones present.

The pitch change test consists of thirty pairs of chords. In some of the pairs, one tone is either higher or lower in the second chord than in the first. A typical change is from major to minor or vice versa. In other pairs the two chords are the same. The subject is to check "U," "D," or "S" for up, down, or same.

The memory test contains thirty pairs of melodies ranging in length from three to ten tones. The second melody of each pair is like the first, except that one tone is altered, and the subject must indicate the number of the altered tone. He is instructed that if no tone is altered he should write "S" for same, but there are no unaltered melodies and no blanks for "S" responses.

The fourth, fifth, sixth, and seventh tests are of rhythmic accent, harmony, intensity, and phrasing. The subject must indicate whether he prefers the first or second version of a short melody, if they differ, or whether the two are the same. There are fourteen items in each test.

The answer sheet contains a few questions concerning the musical background of the subject and his family. The battery yields a score for each of the seven tests and a total score. However, the author suggests that the last four tests may be omitted, particularly with younger children, and the first three used by themselves. The first three tests measure aural acuity, and the last four measure both acuity and taste.

The manual contains norms expressed as letter grades for each year of age from 8 through 17 (adult) for the total scores on the seven tests and for the total scores on the first three tests. The battery was designed to select talented students 10 or 11 years of age, but the author reports that it has been used successfully with children as young as age 7. Wing, former principal of the City Training College in Sheffield, England, also gives a formula for calculating the "musical age" of the pupil.

The author claims a reliability for the battery of .90 or above for older

* Herbert D. Wing. 1939, 1948, 1957, 1960, 1961. National Foundation for Educational Research (England and Wales), The Mere, Upton Park, Slough, Buckinghamshire, England. Age 8 through adult. $14 per set, including manual, 7½ ips half-track tape, scoring stencils, and 20 answer sheets. 60 minutes.

children and .70 for younger children. McLeish reports individual test reliabilities ranging from .65 to .86, with a reliability for the total score of .90 (6:345). Wing claims a validity of .73, based on the *Aliferis Music Achievement Test* with college students, but a validity of only .60 with 11-year-olds, based upon teacher ratings. Inasmuch as one purpose of the battery was to predict success in instrumental training, the author sought to validate the tests by determining the percentage of below-average, average, and above-average students who gave up the study of an instrument. He found these percentages to be 40, 27, and 2 for adolescent boys and 83, 30, and 9 for adults.

The battery is based on an omnibus approach, reflecting Wing's belief that there exists a general factor of musical talent. The tests have been carefully prepared, with the result that the Wing battery represents one of the better instruments available today for the measurement of musical ability. Perhaps its most serious limitation is the technical quality of the tape. Also, when the test items are supposed to be the same, it would be better to re-use the original master recording of the excerpt than to ask the performer to play the excerpt again in an identical manner. The battery deserves to be re-recorded in order that it can be of maximum benefit to music instructors and psychologists. The reliability and validity should be investigated further, and percentile norms, though less frequently used in Britain than in this country, should be made available.

American users might find it interesting if norms for American children were provided, particularly since many of the melodies used in the preference tests are British folk songs. However, there is no evidence to contradict Wing's claim that the familiar melodies are as difficult as the unfamiliar ones.

CONRAD INSTRUMENT-TALENT TEST*

The Conrad battery consists of tests of pitch, tempo, rhythm, harmony, and tone recognition. Each test contains five items. All items are played by the examiner on the piano or administered by means of an electric metronome. In the rhythm test the student must indicate whether a tempo remains constant or whether it varies. The harmony test requires the pupil to check which of two chords sounds better; in each case the "better" chord is a major triad, and in one instance the "poorer" chord is a minor triad. In the tone recognition test, the subject is given a tone and asked to count the number of times that tone appears in a four-measure melody.

Instructions are included for classifying the student according to the structure of his hands, lips, and jaws. In addition, the pupil is asked to indicate what kind of music he likes best and in which subjects he receives the best grades. All the information obtained is combined by means of charts to indicate which specific instrument or instruments the

* Jacques W. Conrad. 1941. Mills Music, Inc., 1619 Broadway, New York, N. Y. 10019. Age 6 through adult. $3 per set, including manual and 100 answer sheets. 25 minutes.

pupil is best suited to study. The determination of the best instrument for the individual is the primary purpose of the battery. The author assumes that there is an instrument suitable for every child.

No data concerning reliability or validity are given, and the author appears to have given little thought to technical considerations. Most instrumental teachers will accept the importance of certain physical characteristics in playing certain instruments, but the author presents no information to substantiate his implicit claim that relationships exist between abilities in English and tonal recognition, arithmetic and tempo, and geography and harmony. The battery cannot be considered a serious predictive instrument.

TILSON-GRETSCH
MUSICAL APTITUDE TEST*

The Tilson-Gretsch battery includes tests of pitch, intensity, time, and tonal memory. The answer sheets are scored by hand. Although there is no manual, norms for grades 4–6, 7–9, and 10–12 are printed on the scoring stencil. The accuracy of the recording of the pitch test is unsatisfactory, but the intended deviations are so large that technical accuracy is probably not a limiting factor. There is a high level of background noise throughout the recording.

The author claims that the battery has a retest reliability of .83 and a validity of .50, based on performance marks in grades 4 through 12. It is questionable that a meaningful validation can be achieved by using marks from such diverse levels, and the issue is clouded still further when one considers what the performance marks may be based on.

The instructions are included on the recording, but the lack of a manual is unfortunate.[5] The test is strongly promotional in nature and is designed, at least in part, to create interest in the study of musical instruments. Though listed at $6.95, the test materials are usually supplied free of charge through a local music store. A number of such tests are available, but this is the only one that is standardized. The use of these tests may be justified when the instructor realizes their purposes and limitations, but one must not confuse a promotional test with a serious psychometric device. The reference on the recording to "those . . . who pass the test" is puzzling and regrettable.

Perhaps because of the nature of the battery, the test items tend to be easy and to lack discriminating power. According to the rating chart printed on the scoring stencil, a score of 76 is "excellent," though it corresponds to a high school percentile rank of only 37. Further, the instructor is told that scores from 40 to 60 are "average," though at the high school level these scores represent percentile ranks of 2 and 9. It is

---

* Lowell M. Tilson. 1941. The Fred. Gretsch Mfg. Co., 218 S. Wabash Ave., Chicago, Ill. 60604. Grades 4-12. $6.95 per set, including 33⅓ rpm recording, scoring stencil, and 100 answer sheets. 60 minutes.

[5] A reprint of an article by Tilson (61), which serves as a manual, is furnished by the publisher on request.

a curious statistical paradox when only 1 per cent of the examinees score below "average" and 90 per cent score above. Although the Tilson-Gretsch battery is easier and probably more interesting for young children than the Seashore battery, it is severely limited as a prognostic tool.

(GASTON) TEST
OF MUSICALITY*

The first page of Gaston's answer sheet consists of a self-rating questionnaire, in which the student checks "yes" or "no" to a series of questions concerning his liking for various musical activities and the importance of music in his home environment. The last page of the four-page answer sheet provides space for the teacher to rate the student on health, attendance, and physical and personality characteristics.

In each of the first five items, the pupil hears a tone and a chord and must check "yes" or "no" depending upon whether or not the tone is present in the chord. In the next five items, the pupil is to compare the melody he hears with the notation printed on his answer sheet. He is to check whether the two versions are the same, whether the notes are different, or whether the rhythm is different.

In the third portion of the examination, there are five melodies in which the final tone is missing, and the student is asked to check whether the final tone should be higher or lower than the last tone heard. The last portion of the examination consists of seven melodies, each of which is repeated from two to six times. The student is to indicate whether each repetition is the same as the original, whether it differs in notes, or whether it differs in rhythm. To remember a melody throughout a series of modified versions demands a tonal memory of a higher order than that required by many tonal memory tests.

The Gaston test is based not upon sensory perception but rather upon perception in a musical context. The instrument used is the piano. Gaston's approach to musicality, like Wing's, is essentially that of Mursell rather than that of Seashore. His materials are musical in character. Consequently, the test is more interesting to students and more appealing to music educators, but it may also be more vulnerable to the effects of musical training and experience.

The author reports split-half reliabilities of .88 for grades 4–6 and for grades 7–9, and .90 for grades 10–12. These coefficients are high in view of the brevity of the test. As evidence of validity he applies a test of significance to the assumption that only a random relationship exists between test scores and teacher ratings. This null hypothesis, it was found, may be rejected at the .03 level for grades 10–12, at the .10 level for grades 4–6, and at the .05 level for all grades, 4–12, combined. Norms are presented for boys and girls separately by grades in steps of one or two

* E. Thayer Gaston. 1942, 1950, 1956, 1957. Odell's Instrumental Service, 925 Massachusetts St., Lawrence, Kansas 66044. Grades 4-12. $10 per specimen set, including manual, 33⅓ rpm recording, scoring stencil, and 1 answer sheet; additional answer sheets, 5¢ each. 30 minutes.

grades from 4 through 12 and by ages in steps of one to three years from 9 through 18.

The *Test of Musicality* is carefully constructed and well standardized, although it would be helpful if the scoring of the self-rating portion could be simplified and more validity data presented. The test deserves wider use and experimentation than it has received thus far.

KWALWASSER MUSIC TALENT TEST*

In the *Kwalwasser Music Talent Test*, a melodic pattern of three notes is immediately repeated with an alteration in either rhythm, pitch, time, or loudness. The answer sheet lists two of these characteristics for each item, and the subject must indicate which of the two characteristics is altered. All of the tones are produced electronically.

A set of norms for grades 4 through 6 is supplied with Form B, while Form A includes one set of norms for junior high school and another set for high school and college combined. The manual contains no specific instructions for administering the test and, amazingly, no data whatever on either reliability or validity. Farnsworth reports a reliability of only .48 (5:384), and it appears that technically the test is unmistakably deficient. Brevity and simplicity appear to be its sole virtues.

DRAKE MUSICAL APTITUDE TESTS**

The *Drake Musical Aptitude Tests* comprise a musical memory test and a rhythm test. Each of these consists of two forms, Form A and Form B. The musical memory test was first published in 1934 and was available separately until 1954, when it was incorporated with the rhythm test in the *Drake Musical Aptitude Tests*. The answer sheets are scored by hand, and the process is complicated somewhat by the lack of scoring stencils.

The two forms of the musical memory test are equivalent, and the author suggests that in testing persons with five or more years of musical experience either Form A or Form B be omitted. With less experienced subjects, however, both forms should be used. In the musical memory

* Jacob Kwalwasser. 1953. Mills Music, Inc., 1619 Broadway, New York, N. Y. 10019. Grades 4-6; 7 through adult. Form A (grade 7 through adult) and Form B (grades 4-6) (nonequivalent). $4.75 per set for each form, including manual, 33⅓ rpm recording, scoring stencil, and 100 answer sheets. 15 minutes.

** Raleigh M. Drake. 1954, 1957. Science Research Associates, Inc., 259 E. Erie St., Chicago, Ill. 60611. Age 8 through adult. Forms A and B (equivalent for musical memory test; nonequivalent for rhythm test). $6.95 per specimen set, including manual, 33⅓ rpm recording, and 1 each of the 2 answer sheets; additional answer sheets for the musical memory test, $6 per 100; additional answer sheets for the rhythm test, $6 per 100. 20 minutes for one form of either test; 80 minutes for both forms of both tests.

test, the examinee hears a recorded melody played on the piano. The melody is then repeated from two to seven times. For each repetition the subject must indicate by marking "S," "K," "T," or "N" whether the repetition is the same as the original, whether the key has been changed, whether the time (rhythm) has been changed, or whether the notes have been changed. There are twelve melodies, with a total of fifty-four repetitions in each test form.

The two forms of the rhythm test are not equivalent. Form B is more difficult. In testing persons with five or more years of musical experience, the author suggests using only Form B. In testing unselected groups both forms should be used.

In the rhythm test the subject hears a metronome establish a tempo while a voice counts with the metronome, "one, two, three, four." Both the metronome and the voice are then silent, and the examinee is to continue counting to himself in the same tempo until the voice says "stop." The number the student is counting at the moment the voice says "stop" is his answer. The test measures the student's ability to maintain a constant tempo. There are fifty items on each form. In Form B the task is complicated by having the metronome on the recording beat in a different tempo during the interval the subject is counting to himself.

Split-half reliabilities of .91 to .93 for musical subjects and .85 for nonmusical subjects are reported for the musical memory test. For the rhythm test, reliabilities for musical subjects range from .83 to .95 for Form A and from .69 to .96 for Form B. For nonmusical subjects the range is from .56 to .89 for Form A and from .69 to .88 for Form B. Validity coefficients, based upon teacher ratings, are presented for several groups of subjects. For the musical memory test, the range is from .32 to .91, with a median of .55. For the combined forms of the rhythm test, the range is from .31 to .85, with a median of .58.

Drake's reported correlations between his rhythm test and Seashore's, which range from .02 to .11, suggest that the two tests do not measure the same traits and that test authors have not yet agreed on a uniform system of terminology. Drake's test would more appropriately be called a test of tempo, as he acknowledges in his manual.

For the rhythm test percentile norms are provided for musical and nonmusical subjects for each form and for the combined forms. For the musical memory test, similar norms are provided by two-year steps from ages 7-8 to ages 19-20 or 21-22.

The battery is sound statistically and psychologically, but the validity picture is obscure. The wide range of validity r's based on teacher ratings may be less a reflection on the Drake battery than on the ability of teachers to rate their students. The battery measures only two aspects of musical ability, and some critics have contended that the ability to maintain a steady tempo in the presence of a distracting tempo is less important than several other abilities involving time and rhythm. Nevertheless, Drake's battery is well prepared and well standardized. It must be regarded as an important positive step in the direction of the satisfactory identification of musical talent.

(GORDON) MUSICAL
APTITUDE PROFILE*

The *Musical Aptitude Profile* contains three tests: Tonal Imagery (Part I, Melody; Part II, Harmony); Rhythm Imagery (Part I, Tempo; Part II, Meter); and Musical Sensitivity (Part I, Phrasing; Part II, Balance; Part III, Style). The answer sheets may be scored either by hand or by machine through the publisher's scoring service. Each test item consists of a musical "statement" followed by an "answer" of equal length. In the melody portion of the tonal imagery test, the answer may be a melodic variation of the statement, resulting from the addition of embellishing notes, or it may be a different melody. The subject is asked to indicate whether, if the added tones were removed, the answer would be like the statement or different from it. There are forty items. In the harmony portion a bass line played by the cello is added to the melody line played by the violin. The subject must indicate whether, if the added tones were removed, the lower voice of the answer would be the same as or different from the lower voice of the statement. The upper voice is the same in each of the forty pairs.

Both portions of the rhythm imagery test are played on the violin. In the first portion the tempo of the statement is kept constant while the tempo of the answer may accelerate, retard, or remain constant. The subject is to indicate whether the tempo of the answer is the same as or different from that of the statement. Each part of the rhythm imagery test contains forty items. In the meter portion of the test, the subject is asked to indicate whether the answer is like the statement or different from it with respect to the accents that determine the meter.

The phrasing portion of the musical sensitivity test is played by the violin and cello, while the balance and style portions are played by the violin alone. Each portion contains thirty items. These three subtests are tests of musical preference. The subject is asked to indicate which of two performances of the same excerpt "sounds better." In the phrasing subtest it is phrasing and expression that are varied. In the balance subtest the endings are different, both melodically and rhythmically. In the style subtest the two performances differ primarily in tempo.

The battery yields eleven scores. There are scores for each of the seven subtests, each of the three basic tests, and a composite score. The author claims split-half reliabilities by grades for unselected subjects on the individual subtests ranging from .66 to .85. Reliabilities of composite scores for unselected subjects range from .90 for grade 4 to .96 for grade 11, with a median of .94. All are unusually high. Validity coefficients for homogeneous groups, based upon teachers' ratings and composite test scores,

* Edwin Gordon. 1965. Houghton Mifflin Company, 110 Tremont St., Boston, Mass. 02107. Grades 4-12. $48 per set, including manual, three 7½ ips single-track tapes, 100 machine-scorable answer sheets, scoring stencils, 100 cumulative record file folders, 100 musical talent profiles, and 2 class record sheets. 3 sessions of 50 minutes each.

classified by performance groups, range from .64 for elementary choir students to .97 for junior high boys' glee club, with a median of .79. These also are unusually high. When validated against performance criteria, coefficients ranging from .12 for elementary chorus to .55 for junior high school band, with a median of .29, are shown. These data suggest that the battery compares quite favorably with comparable existing tests, particularly in reliability.

The battery has been standardized for a population of more than 12,000 students. Percentile norms for each subtest are provided for each grade from 4 through 12. In addition, norms are presented for musically select students in grades 4-6, 7-9, and 10-12. Tables are provided for converting raw scores on each subtest into standard scores. Results are reported as profiles of percentile scores on the three basic tests together with the composite score. Forms are provided for reporting this information to students and parents, and cumulative record folders for each student are also furnished.

The *Musical Aptitude Profile* is unique in several respects. First, the stimuli are produced by string instruments; previous tests have used piano or electronically produced tones. Second, the examples were recorded by well-known artist performers. Third, the manual includes specific teaching suggestions for use with students who score high and students who score low on each of the seven subtests.

Critics may complain that the battery is too long and too complicated, that the test materials are too expensive, that the terminology employed is inaccurate (for example, in the style subtest it is basically tempo that is varied), that original examples are unlikely to be as musical as examples from recognized works, and that there are no absolute standards for evaluating musical preferences. Yet only by using original examples can one be certain that familiarity will not be an influential factor, and the length of the battery is probably one reason for its high reliability. In technical matters there are no major weaknesses apparent in the battery.

The test manual, spiral-bound with wire, is perhaps the most complete and helpful manual published with any musical aptitude test. Not only are there complete instructions for administering the test, but also there is a particularly useful section devoted to the interpretation of the test results. Another excellent section is devoted to technical considerations. The rationale underlying the test is described objectively, and the claims made for the battery are realistic and free from the extravagant exaggeration that sometimes accompanies such literature.

The *Musical Aptitude Profile* is particularly notable for the thoroughness and care that have characterized its preparation. It is definitely one of the most important contributions to the continuing study of musical aptitude.

(BENTLEY) MEASURES
OF MUSICAL ABILITY*

Bentley's battery contains four recorded tests: pitch discrimination, tonal memory, chord analysis, and rhythmic memory. The tones of the pitch test are produced by an oscillator and the differences range from approximately 100 cents to 12 cents. The tones of the other tests are played on the organ. In the rhythmic memory test, the subject hears a pair of rhythmic patterns and must give the number of the beat on which any difference occurs or he may indicate that the two are the same. The other two tests are similar to the corresponding tests of Wing's. The characteristically British inflection on the recording, as on Wing's, may be distracting to young pupils in the United States.

As a table of norms, the author presents the scores achieved by the top and bottom 10 per cent, the next 20 per cent from the top and bottom, and the middle 40 per cent for each year of age from 7 through 14. He identifies these five groups by the letter grades, A, B, C, D, and E. Bentley believes, as does Wing, that finer distinctions are neither justified nor necessary. Nevertheless, some teachers no doubt will wish that both authors had included percentile norms. A student in the "B" group may differ more from another student in the same group in ability than he does from a student in the "A" group. The competent test user is aware that percentile norms must be interpreted with caution.

A brief, eight-page brochure serves as the test manual. However, Bentley's book (3) describing the development and standardization of the battery constitutes, in a sense, a complete test manual. The author, Senior Lecturer in Music Education at the University of Reading, England, claims a retest reliability of .84 and a validity of .94, based on examination grades in sight singing, melodic and rhythmic dictation, and singing back a melody played by the examiner.

Bentley's is the only adequately standardized aptitude test battery designed exclusively for the elementary grades. Thorough instructions and numerous examples are included on the recording, the number of each item is given, and the battery is brief. Further, the author is reasonable in the claims he makes for his tests and properly cautious in his suggestions regarding interpretation of the scores. Because of the technical adequacy and the unique character of the battery, it should help to fulfill a need felt by many elementary music teachers.

PROMOTIONAL TESTS

In addition to the aptitude tests listed above, several other informal, unstandardized tests allegedly intended to measure the pupil's aptitude for musical study are available

* Arnold Bentley. 1966. October House, Inc., 134 E. 22nd St., New York, N. Y. 10010. Ages 7-12. $8 per set, including manual, 33⅓ rpm recording, scoring key, and 25 answer sheets. 25 minutes.

from instrument manufacturers and dealers. These tests, identified here as promotional tests, are short, easy to administer, easy to take, and inexpensive. They are intended to create interest in the study of musical instruments, and sometimes their administration is closely linked to the promotional activities of music stores. Most of these tests are designed for use from approximately grades 4 through 8, and most are free of charge. Even where charges are shown, the materials are often available free through local dealers. Measures of rhythm, pitch, melody, and chords are typically included. Although such tests are in no sense serious evaluative devices, they can provide approximations of relative ability and may be precisely what is needed by the instrumental instructor under certain circumstances. Some answer sheets provide space for information concerning physical features such as evenness of teeth, thickness of lips, and shape of jaw, which may be helpful in recommending a specific instrument. The following list includes some of the better-known promotional tests, listed alphabetically by title. Most provide no norms and none provide data on reliability and validity.

Advanced Rhythm and Pitch Test by C. L. McCreery. Lyons Band Instrument Company, Inc., 223 W. Lake St., Chicago, Ill. 60606. No charge.

Elementary Rhythm and Pitch Test by C. L. McCreery. Lyons Band Instrument Company, Inc., 223 W. Lake St., Chicago, Ill. 60606. No charge.

Leblanc Music Talent Quiz, edited by E. C. Moore. G. Leblanc Corporation, 7019 Thirtieth Ave., Kenosha, Wis. 53141. $3 per 100.

Meyers Music Aptitude Test. Meyers Music Company, 3448 Grand River Blvd., Detroit, Mich. 48208. No charge.

Music Aptitude Test (formerly known as the *Pan-American Music Aptitude Test*). Conn Corporation, 1101 E. Beardsley Ave., Elkhart, Ind. 46515. Manual, 25¢; answer cards, 50¢ per 100.

Music Talent Test. F. E. Olds and Son, Inc., 7373 N. Cicero Ave., Chicago, Ill. 60646. No charge.

Selmer Music Guidance Survey. H. & A. Selmer, Inc., Box 310, Elkhart, Ind. 46515. Manual, $1.20 per dozen; answer cards, $1 per 100; optional 33⅓ rpm recording, $1.

7

Tests of
Musical Achievement

Musical learning takes many forms. It involves acquiring attitudes, understanding, appreciation, skills, and knowledge. Some aspects of musical learning are extremely elusive and seem to defy concise and comprehensive definition. Of these five important types of learning, only the acquiring of factual knowledge readily lends itself to objective testing. Thus, the nature of music itself is the source of part of the difficulty in evaluation. There is sometimes a wide gap between those matters which are of greatest importance and those matters on which the students can be tested most easily. Because appreciation and understanding are two of the most important goals of the music education program, it is particularly unfortunate that these two of the most difficult aspects of learning to measure.

Another major obstacle to the widespread acceptance of any specific achievement test in music has been the lack of consensus among music teachers as to what specific outcomes should be expected as a result of instruction in music. Concurrently, there has been a lack of agreement on what specific musical experiences and activities should constitute the curriculum, for one can scarcely know how to proceed if he has not identified his goal. The measure of uniformity that does exist among the better elementary programs is in part the result, and in part the cause, of similarities among the leading basic series books. At the secondary level the major unifying force has been the tradition of performing groups. Yet there does not appear to be sufficient unanimity as to what specific behaviors are desired that either an achievement test or a series of achievement tests in music is likely to receive the widespread acceptance accorded certain tests of other types. Further, the situation is complicated somewhat by an underlying prejudice against standardized tests on the part of some music educators, who believe that aesthetic growth, depending as it does largely upon attitude and appreciation, cannot be reduced to quantitative terms as satisfactorily as can growth in subject-matter fields that rely more heavily upon factual information.

An achievement test must be reviewed periodically and revised if necessary so that it can be consistent with contemporary philosophy and curricular content. Some of the achievement tests presently on the market have not been kept current. The publishers of such tests have been negligent, and music educators contemplating the use of older achievement tests should examine the content to make certain that it is in agreement with what they are teaching in their classrooms.

BEACH MUSIC TEST*

The *Beach Music Test* consists of eleven parts, entitled (1) Knowledge of Music Symbols, (2) Recognition of Measure, (3) Tone Direction and Similarity, (4) Pitch Discrimination, (5) Application of Syllables, (6) Time Values, (7) Terms and Symbols, (8) Correction of Notation, (9) Syllables and Pitch Names, (10) Representation of Pitches, and (11) Composers and Artists.

The manual claims split-half reliabilities of .86 for university students and .83 for high school students. No data for younger subjects are presented. Validity coefficients based on teacher ratings of general musicianship vary from .35 to .92, with a median of .65. Validated against teacher ratings of knowledge of music fundamentals, the coefficients range from .14 to .94, with a median of .74. Percentile norms in steps of five percentiles are presented for grades 7 through 12 and for the university level.

The *Beach Music Test* is awkward and time consuming to score. Although it enjoyed considerable popularity at one time, it is now out of date and must be regarded as of historical importance only.

KWALWASSER-RUCH TEST OF MUSICAL ACCOMPLISHMENT**

This battery contains ten subtests: (1) Knowledge of Musical Symbols and Terms, (2) Recognition of Syllable Names, (3) Detection of Pitch Errors in a Familiar Melody, (4) Detection of Time Errors in a Familiar Melody, (5) Recognition of Pitch Names,

* Frank A. Beach. 1920, 1930 (with H. E. Schrammel), 1932, 1939. Bureau of Educational Measurements, Kansas State Teachers College, Emporia, Kansas 66802. Grades 4-16. $1.65 per set, including manual, scoring key, and 25 test booklets. 40 minutes.

** Jacob Kwalwasser and G. M. Ruch. 1925, 1927. Bureau of Educational Research and Service, State University of Iowa, Iowa City, Iowa 52241. Grades 4-12. $6.50 per set, including manual and 100 test booklets. 50 minutes.

(6) Knowledge of Time Signatures, (7) Knowledge of Key Signatures, (8) Knowledge of Note Values, (9) Knowledge of Rest Values, and (10) Recognition of Familiar Melodies from Notation.

Decile norms are provided for each grade from 4 through 8 and for grades 9 through 12 combined. The authors claim a surprising split-half reliability of .97 for the battery. Other than a reference to the 1921 recommendations of the Music Educators National Conference (14), not all of which are reflected in the test, no validity data are presented.

The title promises more than the test actually delivers. As a test of musical notation, this battery appears to have high face validity. Yet familiarity with notation is not synonymous with musical accomplishment. It is not an end but a means to an end. In fact, one might question whether any battery that confines itself to paper-and-pencil items, excluding actual music, can properly be called an achievement test in music. The instructor who accepts this score alone as an adequate measure of musical accomplishment is making a serious error.

KWALWASSER TEST
OF MUSIC INFORMATION
AND APPRECIATION*

The *Kwalwasser Test of Music Information and Appreciation* contains nine subtests dealing with music history, biography, instrumentation, and form.

A three-page, mimeographed "manual" provides a single set of percentile norms but, disappointingly, no information whatever as to reliability or validity. Reliabilities of .84 and .70 to .72 have been reported by Farnsworth (18:165) and by Woody (68:36) respectively, but it is difficult to account for the omission of such data by the author. The test is tedious to score.

Kwalwasser's battery demonstrates why a test of music information must be revised periodically. Some of the information required is no longer current. Those few students who recognize the name of Hans Kindler would no doubt identify him as a conductor rather than as a cellist, which he was in his earlier years, and which the key indicates to be the correct answer. Other information is no longer widely taught. Probably only a small minority of American pupils today could identify the nationality of the composer Sinding (Scandinavian), name the composer of "From the Land of the Sky-Blue Water" (Cadman), or identify the orchestral family to which the ophicleide belongs (brass-wind). Still other items are either ambiguous or incapable of being answered simply. For example, among the true-false statements, one finds, "The bass-tuba is considered a solo instrument" (false, according to the key); "The euphonium has two 'bells' or 'flares'" (true); "Ultra modern music follows a strict form" (false); and "A *sonatina* is a small sonata" (true).[1]

* Jacob Kwalwasser. 1927. Bureau of Educational Research and Service, State University of Iowa, Iowa City, Iowa 52241. Grades 9-16. $5 per set, including manual and 100 test booklets. 45 minutes.

[1] Used by permission. Bureau of Educational Research and Service. State University of Iowa.

The title of the test is of doubtful appropriateness. *Kwalwasser Test of Music Information* would be much more fitting. The test deals with factual information about music, musicians, and instruments, and there are few items that could be said to measure an individual's appreciation of music. The continued publication of the battery in its present form can scarcely be justified.

KNUTH ACHIEVEMENT TESTS IN MUSIC*

Each form of the Knuth battery consists of 120 aural musical phrases of four measures each, based on an analysis of the basic series books current at the time the tests were written. The notation for the first two measures is given, and the student must select the notation for the final two measures from among four alternatives. The battery is organized in three divisions of forty items each, one for grades 3-4, one for grades 5-6, and one for grades 7-12. There are two equivalent forms for each division.

The Knuth tests have recently been re-issued on tape and filmstrips. The earlier edition required the examiner to play the examples on the piano while the student compared the auditory stimulus with the printed notation in his answer booklet.

The title is excessively encyclopedic, for the battery actually measures only one aspect of musical achievement, namely, the ability to associate musical notation with aural stimuli. This function is performed quite adequately, but the examiner must not accept the score as a comprehensive measure of the student's achievement in music.

The author claims an equivalent-forms reliability of .96 with college freshmen. Validity is based largely upon the collective judgment of a small group of experts and on an analysis of elementary series. Percentile norms are based upon a population of more than 10,000 students. Norms for certain performing media and organizations are also provided. Scores are corrected for guessing. As the oldest music achievement test still feasible for general use, the Knuth battery makes possible comparisons between today's pupils and their counterparts of more than a quarter of a century ago.

STROUSE MUSIC TEST**

The *Strouse Music Test* consists of two sections, called divisions, each of which contains nine parts or subtests. The musical examples are to be played on the piano or, according to the manual, if no piano is available, they may be sung. Division One is composed of aural exercises, and Division Two consists largely of true-false and multiple-choice items concerned with facts about music.

* William E. Knuth. 1936, 1966. Creative Arts Research Associates, 30 Cedro Way, San Francisco, Calif. 94132. Grades 3-4, 5-6, 7-12. Forms A and B (equivalent). $19.50 per set for each form, including two 7½ ips single-track tapes, manual, filmstrip, scoring stencil, and 100 machine-scorable answer sheets. 45 minutes for each division.

** Catherine E. Strouse, edited by H. E. Schrammel. 1937. Bureau of Educational Measurements, Kansas State Teachers College, Emporia, Kansas 66802. Grades 4-16. Forms A and B (equivalent). $1.65 per set, including manual, scoring keys, and 25 test booklets. 60 minutes.

The author claims reliabilities of .94 for grade 7, .95 for grade 9, and .90 for university students. As evidence of validity she suggests that the content was selected "to meet the basic objectives in public school music" and that the "criticisms and suggestions" of competent teachers and supervisors were considered. She claims a correlation of .90 between Form A of the *Strouse Music Test* and the *Kwalwasser-Ruch Test of Musical Accomplishment*. Although not startling in view of the similarity between the two in philosophy and technique, the correlation is evidence of validity only if one accepts the Kwalwasser-Ruch test as valid.

The *Strouse Music Test* attempts to include more than one can reasonably expect in so brief a measure. As a result the sampling in several of the subtests is inadequate. Of the nine parts of Division One, two contain one item each, two contain two items, and four contain three items.

Percentile norms in steps of five percentiles are provided for each grade from 4 through 8. There is also a set for grades 9 through 12 and another for college freshmen. Although the test booklets themselves are printed, the instructions to the examiner and the scoring keys are mimeographed. The test is unnecessarily difficult to score.

The most conspicuous limitation of the *Strouse Music Test*, however, is the arbitrary and ambiguous nature of some of the true-false and multiple-choice items. For example, "The alto instrument of the string quartet is the: 1. violin, 2. 'cello, 3. viola, 4. string bass" (answer: number 1). Another item requires identification of a 1¼-in. curved line as indicating either a (1) slur, (2) phrase mark, (3) tie, or (4) faster tempo. There is no notation except the curved line, and, though the scoring key gives number 2 as the answer, numbers 1 and 3 must be considered equally correct.

The true-false portions contain other faulty examples. "A rondo is a round in musical form." Youngsters who know what a rondo is but who associate the term "round" with canons such as "Row, Row, Row Your Boat" may easily miss this item, allegedly true. "The March is frequently written in 4-4 measure" (true). Here the student is required to interpret the word "frequently," which may lead him into error if his experience has been largely with military marches in *alla breve* or 6-8 meter. "Schumann-Heink was known as the world's most beloved soprano" (false; she was an alto).[2] This item, ill-founded originally, becomes even more unfair as time passes. Because of the number of ambiguous and arbitrary items on this test, it is of little use today.

ALIFERIS MUSIC ACHIEVEMENT TEST (COLLEGE ENTRANCE LEVEL)*

In the *Aliferis Music Achievement Test*, the student must choose which of three or four written alternatives

[2] Used by permission. Bureau of Educational Measurements, Kansas State Teachers College, M. W. Sanders, Director.

* James Aliferis. 1947, 1949, 1950, 1954. University of Minnesota Press, Minneapolis, Minn. 55455. Grades 12-13. $3.75 per specimen set, including manual, scoring key, and 1 test booklet; additional test booklets, $3 per 20; optional 7½ ips single-track tape, $9.50. 45 minutes.

corresponds to the auditory stimulus presented. The test is designed for use with entering freshmen music students at the college level.

There are six subtests: melodic elements, melodic idioms, harmonic elements, harmonic idioms, rhythmic elements, and rhythmic idioms. In the melodic elements test, the subject must choose the melodic interval heard from among four printed in the test booklet. Each of the four alternatives begins with the same note.

In the melodic idioms test, the examinee hears a four-note melody. The first three notes are given in the test booklet, but the fourth must be selected from among four alternatives. Each of the melodic tests contains thirteen items.

In the harmonic elements test, the subject must select the chord he hears from among four choices in the test booklet. Each chord has four voices, and the choices for each item have the same note in the soprano. There are ten items.

The harmonic idioms test consists of eight series of three-chord progressions. The subject is asked to identify which of three alternatives is the one he has heard. The soprano and bass lines are the same for each of the choices in a given item.

In the rhythmic elements test, there are twelve items, each consisting of four basic rhythmic figures. The subject must choose which rhythmic figure is the one he has heard. The basic rhythmic figure is played three times successively, and it appears in a melodic context.

The final test, rhythmic idioms, consists of eight items. In each item the subject must choose the rhythmic figure he hears from among three rhythmic figures of one measure each. Again, the figure is played three times consecutively in a melodic context.

The battery yields four scores. The two melodic tests are totaled for a single score, as are the two harmonic tests and the two rhythmic tests. In addition, these three scores are totaled for a composite score. The test booklet contains a student data sheet with space for information concerning applied music study, theoretical study, and performing experience. The test is scored by hand.

The stimuli may be presented on the piano by the examiner, or they may be presented by means of a tape available from the publisher. The author wisely recommends the use of the tape in order to assure uniformity in presentation and, consequently, maximum reliability.

The author claims reliabilities of .84 for the melodic section, .72 for the harmonic section, .67 for the rhythmic section, and .88 for the total score. As evidence of predictive validity, Aliferis cites a correlation of .53 between test scores and two-year grade-point averages for music students in music courses. When four-year grade-point averages are considered, a correlation of .66 is obtained.

The manual presents norms for each of the three sections of the test and for the total for state universities, private universities, liberal arts colleges, teachers' colleges, and urban conservatories. It also presents norms for each section of the test as well as for the total for four major geographical regions of the United States, East, Midwest, South, and West. In addition there are national norms for the three sections of the test and for the total scores.

The Aliferis test is well constructed and well standardized. Yet, as the author emphasizes, auditory-visual discrimination is but one aspect of musical achievement.

JONES MUSIC
RECOGNITION TEST*

Part I of the *Jones Music Recognition Test* consists of 80 matching items for elementary and junior high school students, and Part II consists of 100 matching items for senior high school and university students. Harmonized musical excerpts, usually four measures in length, are played on the piano by the examiner and must be matched with the correct titles. A recorded presentation would have been preferable. The items are arranged in groups of 10, each group with 12 titles of vocal or instrumental works provided as possible responses. In Part II the subject is asked, in addition, to supply the name of the composer for each of the titles listed, including those unused in the matching, but the author fails to recognize that some of the titles listed have been used by more than one composer. The scoring is tedious. The following selections are representative of those included: (Part I) "Maryland, My Maryland"; "Bendemeer's Stream"; "O Sole Mio"; "Love Divine All Love Excelling"; (Part II) "Orientale" (Cui); "Goodbye" (Tosti); "Pilgrims' Chorus"; "Pastoral Symphony" from the *Messiah;* and "Flower Song" from *Faust.*

Jones's test is unstandardized, and there is no information on reliability and validity. Its usefulness depends upon the extent to which the selections included comprise a representative sampling of the selections the student is expected to be able to identify.

GRADUATE RECORD
EXAMINATIONS ADVANCED
TESTS: MUSIC**

The *Graduate Record Examination Advanced Tests* are available only through the Institutional Testing Program or the National Program for Graduate School Selection of the Educational Testing Service. These tests are not sold and are not available for general use. Because of their confidential nature and because of the need to protect the security of the tests, they are obtainable only under strictly controlled conditions.

The *GRE Advanced Tests* are designed for use with college seniors and graduate students. They are often administered for purposes of guidance

* Archie N. Jones. 1949. Carl Fischer, Inc., 62 Cooper Sq., New York, N. Y. 10003. Grades 4-8, 9-16. Part I (for elementary and junior high schools) and Part II (for senior high schools and colleges). $4.25 per set, including manual, 30 test booklets for Part I, and 30 test booklets for Part II. 45 minutes for Part I; 60 minutes for Part II.

** 1951, revised biennially. Educational Testing Service, Princeton, N. J. 08540. Grade 16 (adult). 180 minutes.

and placement or as qualifying examinations to students beginning graduate work. Music is one of twenty-two fields of study in which examinations are currently available.

Major emphasis in the music examination is on history and literature, though there are also sections dealing with theory, instrumentation and orchestration, and music fundamentals. The papers are scored by the Educational Testing Service, and the scores are reported to the institutions and to the students involved. The cost for taking one advanced test is $2.50 in the Institutional Testing Program or $8 in the National Program for Graduate School Selection.

The Educational Testing Service claims a reliability of .96 for the *Advanced Music Test*. A validity study is under way but is not yet completed. In recognition of the importance of the auditory aspects of music, a 45-minute aural supplement to the *Advanced Music Test* was made available on an experimental basis in 1964.

The test is well constructed. It is also difficult. As a measure of the scholarly aspects of music and, to a lesser extent, the aural aspects of music theory, the *GRE Advanced Music Test* is unequalled. Because of its limited nature, however, it cannot be used alone to evaluate a student's preparation in specialized fields such as composition, performance, music education, or conducting. It is unfortunate that there exist no comparable tests in most of these fields.

ALIFERIS-STECKLEIN
MUSIC ACHIEVEMENT TEST
(COLLEGE MIDPOINT LEVEL)*

This battery, designed for use in colleges and universities at the end of the sophomore year or the beginning of the junior year, resembles its companion test intended for entering freshmen. Like the entrance level test, it may be administered either by tape or by playing the exercises on the piano. The battery includes a melodic interval test of 34 items, a chord test of 26 items, and a rhythm test of 19 items.

In the melodic interval test, the student hears a sequence of four tones. The first three notes are given in the test booklet, along with four choices, from which the subject must select the final note.

The chord test contains major and minor triads, diminished and augmented chords, and various seventh and ninth chords. The subject sees a four-note chord and hears a four-note chord, one note of which is different. He must answer "S," "A," "T," or "B," indicating whether the discrepancy is in the soprano, alto, tenor, or bass. The criticism that the test is unfair because it requires absolute pitch is unjustified because the three correct tones provide a context for the fourth tone. Some of the items

* James Aliferis and John E. Stecklein. 1952, 1954, 1956, 1957, 1962. University of Minnesota Press, Minneapolis, Minn. 55455. Grades 14-15. $3.75 per specimen set, including manual, scoring key, and 1 test booklet; additional test booklets, $3 per 20; optional 7½ ips single-track tape, $9.50. 45 minutes.

appear to have been made more difficult than necessary through enhar-
monic spellings, but the authors provide data showing that each item is
marked correctly by at least 40 per cent of the subjects.

In the rhythm test the subject must locate the rhythmic discrepancy between a six-beat aural example and a six-beat pattern in the test booklet.
As on the entrance level test, the rhythmic exercises are played in melodic
patterns, but the notation in the test booklet is on a single line.

The authors claim a reliability of .92 for the battery and reliabilities of
.90, .84, and .69 for the three subtests respectively. The rhythm test appears to be weak in discriminating power as well as low in reliability. The
authors claim a validity of .41, based on four-year grade-point averages in
all courses. The test manual presents T-scores and percentile scores both
for the subtests and for the battery for students at state universities, private universities, teachers' colleges, state colleges, private colleges, conservatories associated with academic institutions, and independent conservatories. Similar norms are provided for the eastern, midwestern, south-
ern, and western geographical regions of the nation. In addition, norms
are provided for woodwind, brass, string, percussion, piano, and voice
students.

Like the entrance level test, the midpoint test is well constructed and
useful in measuring an important aspect of musical development. The test
is quite specialized and thus is limited in its application. However, it
accomplishes well what it sets out to do and could not be so successful in
this respect if it were less limited.

FARNUM MUSIC
NOTATION TEST*

The test consists of forty melodic
phrases of four measures each, presented on a 78 rpm recording of medio-
cre quality. The pupil has the notation for each example before him in the
test booklet. In one measure of each phrase, the aural version differs from
the printed version in pitch or rhythm. The student checks the appropriate
box indicating the number of the measure in which the aural and visual
stimuli are not in agreement.

Farnum's test is designed for use in the junior high school. Separate
norms are provided for students who have studied instrumental music,
students who have not, and the combined group. Within each of these
classifications, norms are provided for grades 7, 8, and 9, and within each
grade level separate norms are provided for boys and girls. One might
expect that a student guessing at random would answer 10 of the 40 items
correctly inasmuch as there are four possible responses. According to the
norms, however, 16 per cent of the seventh-grade girls who have not taken
lessons fail to do even this well. Further, if an untrained seventh-grade

* Stephen E. Farnum. 1953. The Psychological Corporation, 304 E. 45th St., New York, N. Y.
10017. Grades 7-9. $6.75 per set, including manual, 78 rpm recording, scoring stencil, and 50
test booklets. 20 minutes.

girl can answer four of the remaining 30 items above her chance score, she will rank in the upper half of her group.

The test is short and easy to administer. Split-half reliabilities range from .78 for eighth-grade boys to .91 for ninth-grade boys and girls. As evidence of predictive validity, the author cites three studies showing correlations of .42, .52, and .61 between the *Farnum Music Notation Test* and the *Watkins-Farnum Performance Scale*, administered six to nine months later. Inasmuch as a number of other factors are involved in achieving high scores on the latter test, its use as a validating criterion is open to question. Its author considers the *Farnum Music Notation Test* to be an indicator of readiness for instrumental study, though many directors consider familiarity with notation as measured by this test to be less important than a number of other abilities.

NATIONAL TEACHER EXAMINATIONS: MUSIC EDUCATION*

The *National Teacher Examinations* consist of two major divisions, the "Common Examinations," which include professional education and general education, and the "Teaching Area Examinations." The "Teaching Area Examinations" are designed to measure the level of preparation in specific subject-matter fields, one of which is music education. The tests are intended for college seniors, graduate students, and in-service teachers. The test scores are used, normally in conjunction with other measures, for selecting or certifying new teachers, evaluating the potential of experienced teachers before promotion or awarding of tenure, assigning teachers, and identifying strengths and weaknesses for purposes of in-service training.

The *National Teacher Examinations* are confidential examinations not available for general use or inspection. They may be taken only at specified examination centers on specified dates. The papers are scored by the Educational Testing Service, and scores are reported to the examinee and to the agencies he designates. The cost to the student taking one "Teaching Area Examination" is $7.

The "Teaching Area Examinations" are prepared by panels of specialists nominated by professional organizations. The original *Music Education* examination was prepared in 1957 by a panel of five eminently well-qualified members of the Music Educators National Conference, and the examination was reviewed in detail in 1965 by a similar panel. The Educational Testing Service relies on these procedures in the development of the examinations to insure content validity. Percentile norms are provided for each of the "Teaching Area Examinations" and for the *NTE* composite scores.

The *Music Education* examination, which contains 125 multiple-choice items and is claimed to have a reliability of .89, is based upon the assump-

* 1957, revised annually except 1961, 1962. Educational Testing Service, Princeton, N. J. 08540. Grade 16 (adult). 105 minutes.

tion that the teacher should be familiar with all phases of music teaching from the elementary school through the high school. There are questions dealing with elementary general music, junior high school choir, senior high school orchestra, and so forth. The breadth of the examination constitutes its greatest limitation. Few teachers are competent in all phases of music education, and questions concerning the instrumentation of the high school band, for example, contribute little to the assessment of the qualifications of the elementary vocal teacher. An examination of this nature can be valid only to the extent that the prospective teacher is expected to be able to teach all phases of music at all levels.

Further, the examination is based upon the assumption that there is one correct way to accomplish a given task and that although we must recognize individual differences in students we need not recognize individual differences in teachers. In addition, there are several items on the examination with which one can find fault on grounds of ambiguity.

The Educational Testing Service points out that the tests "do not attempt to measure directly such qualifications as personality, interest in children, or ability to motivate learning," though these factors are pertinent and of utmost importance. Nor do the tests attempt to measure teaching effectiveness or musicianship. The tests provide an objective measure for use when a few teachers are to be chosen from among a large number of applicants, as in a large city system, and to this extent they make it possible to eliminate obvious misfits and avoid arbitrary and capricious judgments. However, unless supplemented by measures of other characteristics, such as sight singing, keyboard proficiency, conducting, or proficiency in a performing medium, the *Music Education* examination cannot be considered an adequate criterion for the employment of music teachers, and its use as a basis for merit salary increases is even more dangerous.

(COLWELL) ELEMENTARY
MUSIC ACHIEVEMENT TESTS*

The Colwell battery consists of two tests. The second is slightly more advanced than the first. The recorded exercises are performed on the piano. The *Elementary Music Achievement Tests* are the only recorded music tests to use a woman's voice. According to the publisher machine-scorable answer sheets will be made available at a later date.

In Test 1 the subject must indicate: (1) whether the second tone of a pair is higher than, lower than, or the same as the first, (2) which of three tones is the lowest, (3) whether a pattern or phrase proceeds scalewise or by leaps, and (4) whether a phrase is in duple or triple meter. The pitch test utilizes a much wider range of pitches than most such tests.

In Test 2 the student must: (1) identify the measures, if any, in which

*Richard Colwell. 1965. Follett Publishing Company, 1010 W. Washington Blvd., Chicago, Ill. 60607. Grades 4-12. $23.07 per set, including manual; 33⅓ rpm recording, 32 answer sheets, and scoring stencil for Test 1; and 33⅓ rpm recording, 32 answer sheets, and scoring stencil for Test 2. 75 minutes.

he finds discrepancies between aural and visual stimuli, (2) indicate which of three tones following a cadence or phrase, if any, corresponds to the keynote established, (3) state whether a pair of chords is major or minor, and (4) indicate whether a phrase is major, minor, or changes from one to the other.

According to the author the test content is based upon the objectives of the elementary music program identified by six leading basic series, and the validity is based upon this relationship. The correlation between test scores and teacher ratings of exceptionally high and low achievers was found to be .92. The author claims a reliability of .94 for Test 1 and .96 for Test 2. Norms for grades 4, 5, 6, 7, 8, and high school are categorized by geographical section of the nation; by size or type of school (i.e., small, suburban, or urban), and by type of instruction (i.e., classroom teacher or music specialist).

The *Elementary Music Achievement Tests* have been carefully constructed. They reflect contemporary thinking with respect to the content of the elementary music program. As the author recognizes, they measure only a limited number of the skills and understandings that comprise the elementary music curriculum. Nevertheless, the *Elementary Music Achievement Tests* represent a most promising attempt to provide an objective measure of the extent to which pupils are acquiring some of the basic skills and concepts music teachers presume they are teaching.

SNYDER KNUTH
MUSIC ACHIEVEMENT TEST*

The Snyder Knuth battery was designed to evaluate the musical background of the college freshman planning to major in elementary education; the author suggests that a student with a raw score of less than 85 should take a music fundamentals course. She also indicates that the battery may be used in the elementary and secondary schools as well as with music majors at the college level, though the only set of norms given is for elementary education majors.

Part I contains forty-six items in which the student hears on tape a brief melody played on the piano and sees the notation on an accompanying filmstrip. At one point in each melody, four alternative versions of the notation are given and the student must choose which is correct. There are also seven items in which he must choose which of four harmonic sequences, indicated by Roman numerals, would be most appropriate to accompany a notated melody.

Thirty-eight aural melodies are presented in Part II. The student must (1) decide which of four contour lines best represents a given melody, (2) determine whether a melody moves by skips, steps, repeated tones, or a combination of these, (3) count the number of times the keynote, the oc-

* Alice Snyder Knuth. 1965. Creative Arts Research Associates, 30 Cedro Way, San Francisco, Calif. 94132. Grades 13-15. Forms A and B (equivalent). $19.50 per set for each form, including two 7½ ips single-track tapes, manual, filmstrip, scoring stencil, and 100 machine-scorable answer sheets. 65 minutes.

tave, or the tonic chord appears in a melody, (4) determine which phrases of a melody are alike, (5) distinguish between duple and triple meter, and (6) distinguish between the major and minor modes.

Part III contains thirty-five items based on relationships between various musical symbols and terms; A is to B as C is to which of four alternatives. A few of these items might more appropriately be cast in another form, such as ordinary multiple-choice.

In Part IV the student is shown the opening phrases of ten well-known melodies, and he must choose which of four titles is the correct one. Parts III and IV involve visual stimuli only.

The author claims a reliability of .99, based on the correlation between the two equivalent forms. As evidence of content validity, she claims that the test items are typical of the material found in basic series books and in curriculums for elementary education majors. Although the norms are only tentative, the battery appears to be useful for screening potential classroom teachers to find those who need a course in music fundamentals.

8

Tests of
Performance
and Appreciation

WATKINS-FARNUM
PERFORMANCE SCALE*

The *Watkins-Farnum Performance Scale*, a test of performance for band instruments, is based upon a scale devised and standardized for the cornet by John G. Watkins in 1942 (65). Watkins examined twenty-three widely used cornet method books to determine the notational symbols used and the order in which they were introduced. On this basis he constructed a set of melodic exercises designed to measure levels of achievement, from the easiest to the most difficult. In the *Watkins-Farnum Performance Scale*, these principles have been adapted to other instruments of the band. The examination is published for cornet and baritone TC; B-flat clarinet, alto clarinet, and bass clarinet; saxophone and oboe; flute; French horn; trombone, baritone BC, and bassoon; tuba; and snare drum. The adaptations for the various instruments consist largely of transpositions and octave adjustments in order to keep the exercises within an appropriate range.

The subject is required to play the fourteen exercises from the test book

* John G. Watkins and Stephen E. Farnum. 1954, 1962. Hal Leonard Music, Inc., 64 E. Second St., Winona, Minn. 55987. For all wind and percussion students. Form A and Form B (equivalent). $6.50 per set (either form), including manual-test book and pad of scoring sheets for the various instruments. Administered individually.

while the examiner marks the errors on a score sheet. Each measure in which an error occurs is marked, and the final score is the number of measures played correctly. The student is stopped when he has played two exercises without scoring. Tempos are indicated by metronomic markings.

The reliability of the test is based partially on the objectivity of the scoring procedure. Errors may involve pitch, time, change of time, expression, slurs, rests, holds and pauses, or repeats. Explicit instructions are provided as to what constitutes an error. Only one error is marked per measure. The beauty of the tone, perhaps the most important criterion of all, is conspicuously missing from the scoring criteria. Although the test is not unreasonably difficult to score, it does place greater demands on the examiner than most other published tests. The examination can be used in testing sightreading or in testing practiced performance.

The authors claim a reliability of .94 for grades 7 through 12 combined, based on equivalent forms. Validity coefficients, based on teacher ratings, vary from .68 for snare drum to .87 for cornet, but the number of subjects involved was very small.

The exercises are designed so that the first will be playable by the pupil who has studied for only a few months; the last will be difficult for the student who has studied for several years. A graph showing the mean raw scores at half-year intervals for a period of six years is presented on the score sheet so that the individual student's score may be compared with the mean. Separate data for the various instruments are not furnished, though the authors acknowledge that differences do exist. Nor are percentile norms provided. For these reasons the test cannot claim to be adequately standardized.

The authors present two tables containing suggested letter grades represented by test scores. The second table is used for oboe, bassoon, French horn, trombone, tuba, and drum students, who were found to score appreciably lower than students on the other instruments. The test requires considerable time to administer because it must be done individually. This disadvantage is inherent in any test of musical performance.

The exercises were prepared in such a way that they present progressively more difficult aspects of musical notation. Such exercises are likely to be somewhat unmusical and artificial in character, as these are. Further, because essentially the same materials are used for each instrument, the exercises are often unidiomatic for some instruments. The tuba and flute, for example, are playing the same exercises. The least the test user could hope for would be separate norms for the various instruments.

Nevertheless, the *Watkins-Farnum Performance Scale* is the only objective test of performance currently available, and, as such, represents an important contribution to music testing. There is clearly a great deal that remains to be done in the measurement of musical performance.

THE CONTEST-FESTIVAL

Competition has been an important part of music education since ancient times, and the music contest was closely related to the unprecedented growth of school music, particularly instrumental music, in the early decades of the present century. As the number of contestants increased, the system of ranking them in order gave way to the group rating plan, whereby each soloist or group is assigned a rating corresponding to a given level of achievement. In this way any number of groups may receive the same rating, and a group is competing against arbitrary standards of excellence rather than against other groups. However, the performance of other groups is a factor in determining what those arbitrary standards are, and the very flexibility that constitutes the principal advantage of the group rating system may at the same time represent its principal disadvantage.

Much of the criticism that has been directed toward the music contest, which is now known more often as the contest-festival or competition-festival, has centered not around the principles involved but around the alleged misapplication of those principles. In an effort to improve the effectiveness of interscholastic music activities, the Music Educators National Conference founded the National Interscholastic Music Activities Commission (NIMAC) as an auxiliary organization in 1952. The *NIMAC Manual* (44), a publication of the Commission, contains suggested policies and practices concerning contest-festivals that, if widely adopted, would aid greatly in standardizing procedures and raising standards.

The interpretation of ratings is often a source of misunderstanding. In most contest-festivals there are five ratings available, but many adjudicators tend to use only the first two. A recent survey of more than 33,000 ratings revealed the following frequency distribution: [1]

Rating	Percentage Awarded
I	38.4
II	45.3
III	16.4
IV	1.3
V	0.1

All groups receiving the same rating should represent approximately the same level of achievement. When fewer ratings are used, groups differing widely in achievement sometimes receive the same rating, a situation unfair to all concerned.

The discrepancies that sometimes occur make it very difficult to compare ratings given at different times and places by different adjudicators. The result is confusion on the part of directors, students, parents, and public. Every adjudicator and every participant should be familiar with the suggested bases for contest ratings published by NIMAC (44:69-70): [2]

Rating I (Division 1), Superior. This division represents the finest conceivable performance for the event and the class of participants being judged; worthy of

[1] M. Orville Johnson, "A Study of the Ratings Received by Missouri High Schools Participating in the District Music Festivals from 1959-1965," *Missouri Journal of Research in Music Education,* I, 5 (1966), 61.

[2] Reprinted with permission. From *NIMAC Manual* (1963), published by the National Interscholastic Music Activities Commission of the Music Educators National Conference, 1201 16th St. N.W., Washington, D. C. 20036.

the distinction of being recognized as among the very best. This rating might be compared to a percentage grade of 95 to 100.

Rating II (Division 2), Excellent. This rating reflects an unusual performance in many respects but not one worthy of the highest rating due to minor defects. Yet it is a performance of distinctive quality. The rating might be compared to a grade of 87 to 94.

Rating III (Division 3), Good. This rating is awarded for a good performance, but one that is not outstanding. The performance shows accomplishment and marked promise, but is lacking in one or more essential qualities. The rating might be compared to a grade of 80 to 86.

Rating IV (Division 4), Fair. This rating describes a performance that shows some obvious weaknesses. These may reflect handicaps in the way of instrumentation or lack of rehearsal time. The rating is comparable to a grade of 75 to 79.

Rating V (Division 5), Below Average. This rating indicates a performance which reveals much room for improvement. The director should check his methods, instrumentation, etc., with those of more mature organizations.

These guidelines represent an attempt to standardize adjudication while at the same time permitting flexibility from one region to another and from one event to another. Though there may be minor variances, attributable to any of a large number of factors, ratings should be assigned and interpreted according to the guidelines established by NIMAC. The age and experience of the individual or group should be considered by the director in choosing appropriate music for the contest-festival, but these factors cannot be used to excuse a totally unsatisfactory or unmusical performance.

NIMAC publishes a set of adjudication forms for all contest-festival events. These forms are widely used, although some state and local organizations prefer to use their own. The criticism offered by the adjudicator must be constructive, and it is essential that the criticism clarify and be consistent with the final rating.

Despite the efforts of NIMAC to standardize and objectify adjudication, the evaluation remains largely a subjective one. A contest-festival is only as good as the adjudication. Those persons charged with selecting the adjudicators have a responsibility for choosing only competent musicians with the background, experience, and temperament for the task. Adjudicators themselves must become familiar with the standards of performance they may expect and avoid being either excessively lenient or excessively harsh. Adjudicators must value musicianship more highly than technique alone, while participating teachers and directors must realize that along with the advantages such a system yields there may also be occasional shortcomings.

THE TRY-OUT
AND CHALLENGE

The terms "try-out" and "audition" refer to procedures for accepting or rejecting students for honors, such as membership in performing organizations, or for seating them in order according to their proficiency. The term "challenge" refers to procedures for revising the order in which they are seated, as the result of a student's claiming greater proficiency than a student seated ahead of him.

Many instrumental directors employ methods in their performing groups whereby students can advance in seating by challenging those above them. Both the amount of emphasis placed on this practice and the administrative details vary considerably, but the pattern worked out over a number of years by Joseph E. Maddy at the National Music Camp at Interlochen, Michigan, represents an excellent example of what can be done. On Friday at each regular section rehearsal, the instructor conducts both try-outs and challenges. He begins the try-outs by choosing a passage in the literature being prepared and asking the first two students, in order, to play it. The other members of the section close their eyes while the two are playing and vote by a show of hands to pick the winner. The instructor may vary the order of playing but even though the students may know who is playing, they do not know who voted for whom. The third player is then asked to play, and again the other members of the section vote whether he should move up a chair. If the vote is affirmative, a vote is taken on whether he should move up two chairs, and so forth. Each player is heard in turn.

When the try-outs have been completed, each student, beginning at the bottom of the section, is given an opportunity to challenge the player ahead. The instructor picks another passage from the literature, and the students play, beginning usually with the one being challenged. Again the members of the section vote with their eyes closed, and, if the challenger is successful, he may immediately challenge the next player and then the next. For each challenge the instructor chooses a different passage. When the student loses, the instructor returns to the bottom of the section and hears the next student. In this way every student has a chance to advance as far as he is able in the section. On some occasions there may be considerable movement within the section, but as time passes the order of the players tends to become more stable. The procedure is familiar to all and requires only a relatively small amount of time. Because considerable prestige is attached to the higher chairs and because no one knows just which passages will be selected, the students are strongly motivated to practice all of the literature in the folders.

Similar systems are used in many instrumental organizations. In few schools does each section have a regular weekly rehearsal, but some conductors are willing to take a limited amount of the rehearsal time of the full ensemble for this purpose. Although not all students thrive on this sort of competition, many directors who use such a system are convinced that it works well and that the increase in motivation and *esprit de corps* justifies the time required. If the director seeks greater anonymity for the students, he may tape the performances in random order and play the tape for the group to judge. Students may be identified by numbers.

Student participation in making the decisions is a valuable feature of this selection process. Not only does it relieve some of the pressure on the instructor, but it is also an excellent training device for the students. It introduces an element of objectivity into an essentially subjective procedure as well.

Rapid evaluation of student performance is frequently necessary in arranging the seating of all-city or all-state groups. Sometimes tentative seating plans are prepared on the basis of recommendations or tapes. Even if no preliminary order has been established, the person in charge of the section can quickly make a rough approximation by listening to each student play the same passage and placing each in the proper order among those who played previously. A tentative arrangement can be verified by having each student in succession play another passage. The student who plays better than the student ahead of him is permitted to move up one chair, and the instructor listens to the next player. This procedure, which represents a variation of the Interlochen system, is then repeated as time allows until one round is completed in which there are no changes. Preferably, the judgments should be made by the members of the section. Moving only one chair at a time tends to minimize the effect of a performance that is not a true reflection of the student's actual ability.

The "jury examination," used by many colleges and universities to examine each applied music student at the close of the term, is an audition given by a committee of the applied music faculty. The music performed normally includes selections from the repertoire the student has prepared during the term. Often scales and arpeggios are also required. The jury examination corresponds to the final examination given in other courses. Frequently, the jury will determine the grade of the student, perhaps with a recommendation from the instructor. In other institutions the jury may recommend a grade but the instructor has the final responsibility.

The professional audition is yet another test of performance, but the procedures vary widely depending upon the nature of the position and upon the person conducting the audition.

THE MEASUREMENT
OF MUSICAL APPRECIATION

Music appreciation is a much abused term. At its best it refers to learning experiences that can provide the student with the most meaningful insights into the true nature of man and art that he will achieve in his lifetime. At its worst it refers to activities that can be an utter waste of time and present a distorted, incomplete view of the art in such a way as to embitter the pupil toward music for the remainder of his life.

Some of the tests described in Chapter 7 were referred to by their authors as appreciation tests. In the broadest sense music appreciation includes knowledge about music and musicians; familiarity with notation, instruments, and musical literature; and acquaintance with historical and technical facts. In a narrower sense, however, music appreciation refers to sensitivity to the aesthetic values of music, and in this sense it is extremely difficult to measure. Some of the major sources of difficulty arise from the following:

1. There are no absolute standards of beauty in music. Neither are there absolute standards of quality. We do not know to what extent aesthetic worth is inherent in a work of art and to what extent it resides in the viewer or listener.

2. Music exists in time. The listener is never in the presence of an entire musical work at one time. He must perceive the meaning of the work by hearing one sonority after another, a disadvantage analogous to that of the art-lover's trying to appreciate a large painting by being shown only one small area at a time.

3. Because of the discursive nature of the art, listening to music demands concentration to an extent perhaps unsurpassed by any other subject-matter field of the curriculum. If the listener allows his mind to wander, even momentarily, he has missed something essential and irretrievable. No such loss is experienced in a test employing only written materials, where the student can go back at any time and read the material again.

4. It is extremely difficult to measure a student's liking for music by means of an objective test because the student often recognizes what the teacher is seeking and responds accordingly. Attempting to measure aesthetic sensitivity may place the teacher in the dangerous position of dictating artistic taste.

5. One of the great assets of music is that its sonorities have no semantic meaning. Music can be anything the individual takes it to be. To impose monolithic values upon such a marvelously flexible expression tends to undermine one of its unique properties.

6. The emotional content and potential of music cannot be evaluated adequately by objective means because these factors are deeply personal. The teacher cannot say what the student's precise emotional reaction should be upon hearing a given musical work. Indeed, the experience of the student may be more intense than that of the teacher.

7. In measuring music appreciation the teacher must concentrate upon the music itself and must not emphasize unduly the programmatic aspects of the music or its extra-musical associations. Primary attention should be directed to the music rather than to facts or stories about it.

8. In measuring aesthetic sensitivity the teacher must be certain that he is using music of aesthetic beauty so that there is something to be sensitive to. This criterion is complicated by the absence of absolute standards of beauty, but few would deny that at least some of the music used in the nation's classrooms is lacking in genuine beauty.

9. The student often does not possess the vocabulary for expressing his understanding or appreciation of music. The development of a technical vocabulary is seldom furthered outside the music classroom and as a result depends largely upon the experience of the student in music classes. It is deplorable if the student with a genuine appreciation of music is penalized in a test of appreciation by his unfamiliarity with technical terms and concepts or by his inability to express himself (190:9-11).

10. Underlying these difficulties is the basic difficulty encountered throughout any discussion of evaluation in music. The outcomes sought must be identified in terms of specific behaviors that can be observed and

evaluated, and the problems involved in attempting to reduce one of man's most profound and moving experiences to a series of true-false or multiple-choice test items are enormous if not insurmountable.

Some writers have suggested that one day we will be able to arrive at an objective mathematical formula that will provide a measure of the degree of beauty present in a work of art. Although it is becoming increasingly hazardous in our society to deny the possible future existence of anything, few aestheticians would be willing to accept this potentiality as likely, if for no other reason than the lack of a standard of beauty. Some argue that to attempt objective measurement of art and artistic appreciation is contrary to the very essence of artistic expression and that due to the introspective, non-verbal nature of music appreciation we shall never be able to measure it any more accurately than we can measure how honest a child is or how much he loves his mother.

THE MUSIC MEMORY
CONTEST

One of the most fascinating chapters in the history of musical testing concerns the music memory contest, a unique rote-learning phenomenon that swept the nation in the 1920's and vanished as quickly as it appeared. In the music memory contest, students were asked to identify by title and composer a wide variety of musical works. The growth of the music memory contest closely paralleled the increased use of the phonograph as a teaching device. Contests were conducted by means of recorded excerpts, some of which were extremely brief and therefore difficult. Responses were written, and students were expected to spell the names of composers correctly.

As a result of enormous popular interest, music memory contests were held throughout the land at the city level, the county level, and even at the state level, with each serving as an elimination round for the next. Although the contest represents a kind of musical learning that would find little professional support today, the success it enjoyed at the peak of its popularity can be explained only in terms of its ability to fulfill an important need felt at that time.

THE MEASUREMENT
OF MUSICAL TASTE

Measures of musical taste normally involve comparing the judgment of the subject with the collective judgment of musical "experts" or with groups from the general population. Such comparisons may be based upon compilations of works programed by major symphonies, works broadcast most frequently on radio and television, best-selling phonograph records, space allotted in reference works, number of times mentioned in scholarly texts, judgments of eminence, or other criteria (16). It is difficult or impossible to establish absolute standards, except when the differences are gross, and the taste of experts as well as the taste of the general population changes from one generation to another. Measures of musical taste may be revealing but are frequently difficult to interpret.

One of the best-known measures of musical taste was the *Oregon Music Discrimination Test*. This test was included in the *Oregon Music Tests*, a battery of five measures developed by Kate Hevner, with the assistance of R. H. Seashore and J. L. Landsbury in 1935 (21, 29). A brief excerpt from a musical work of recognized merit was presented along with a deliberate distortion of the same work by a musical psychologist. There were twelve items each in which the distortion was based on rhythm, harmony, melody, and form. The excerpts were played on the piano and recorded. The subject was asked to indicate which version he preferred and, further, to indicate whether the distortion of the alternate version was in rhythm, harmony, melody, or form. Reliabilities were found to range from .47 for fifth- and sixth-graders to .86 for adults. No item was retained in the test unless its face validity was unanimously confirmed by a panel of musical experts.

A more difficult version, known as Series II, was subsequently added. It consisted of two equivalent forms of forty items each. In Series II, the subject was given the nature of the distortion and was asked not only to pick the original version but to indicate whether he was very sure, fairly sure, or not at all sure of his answer.

The Hevner battery also included the *Oregon Test for Musical Concepts*, in which nine recorded examples of varied musical works were played for the subject. Each was played three times, and the subject was then required to answer a series of true-false questions about the work, e.g., "The first theme begins with an ascending melodic figure," or "The theme is introduced first by the cellos." [3]

THE MEASUREMENT
OF ATTITUDE AND INTEREST

Music appreciation and musical taste are closely related to attitude toward music and interest in music. It would appear that students who are interested in music tend to appreciate it more than those who are not, but the precise nature of the cause-and-effect relationship is not entirely clear. Attempts to measure musical attitude and interest have usually taken the form of either questionnaires or rating scales.

It is difficult to design and interpret measures of attitude and interest. The test author must compose and evaluate his statements strictly on empirical bases. Reliability and validity are exceedingly difficult to determine, and equivalent forms are virtually impossible to construct. As on a personality inventory, there are no right or wrong answers. The subject can often sense what the test writer is seeking and can modify his responses accordingly if he wishes. The examiner must depend upon the

[3] Used by permission. Professor Kate Hevner Mueller, Indiana University.

examinee to be truthful. Curiously, however, the item, "I have never been in trouble with the law," on the *California Psychological Inventory* is marked "true" by 20 per cent of the prison inmates tested (66:123).

The Oregon battery also included a *Test for Attitude Toward Music*, which consisted of fifty statements about music. The subject was asked whether he disagrees, agrees, or strongly agrees with statements such as, "I am against music for I believe the study of it makes people peculiar and narrowminded." There was also a *Self-Rating in Music Training*, in which the subject supplied answers concerning his musical background and study, and a *Self-Rating in Musical Talent*, in which the subject rated himself on a scale from 1 to 10 on such items as, "How well do you sing?" Farnsworth has developed a series of scales for measuring interest in various kinds of music by assigning numerical values for given behavioral characteristics along a line representing a continuum from one extreme to the other (17). Other investigators have designed taste indices in which the subject is asked to complete a series of sentences intended to provide a measure of the individual's taste or attitude toward music. Such measures are difficult to score objectively and require trained personnel for valid interpretation.

General testing programs normally include a number of measures of attitude toward or interest in various fields including music. Two of the best-known tests are the *Kuder Preference Record—Vocational* and the *Strong Vocational Interest Blank*.

THE MEASUREMENT OF MOTOR SKILLS

Some music educators have emphasized the importance of tests of motor control in predicting musical success. The aspect of motor control most frequently tested has been motility, or the ability to perform motor tasks. Motility can be tested by asking the subject to tap on paper with a pencil as many times as he can in five seconds. The score is determined by counting the dots. If the equipment is available, the subject may be asked to tap a telegraph key as many times as possible (46). He may be asked to tongue the syllable "tu" as rapidly as possible. Reaction time also constitutes a measure of motor control, as does the ability of the subject to place needles rapidly into small holes. Such measures may be useful in helping to predict likely success in instrumental performance, a field of study in which coordination and dexterity are essential.

THE MEASUREMENT OF OTHER TRAITS

Instrumental teachers sometimes devise informal measures to indicate the aptitude of students for specific instruments. Examination of the physical features of the student, such as the length of the fingers, the thickness of the lips, and the nature of the dental occlusion, are normally important aspects of this determination. In addition, directors often use a performance test, which may range from a check of the ability to buzz on a cornet mouthpiece to a formal program of several weeks of study on each of a series of instruments (26).

Some writers have stressed the importance of measuring mental imagery. Such a test may be adapted for any of the senses. In a test of auditory or musical imagery, the subject may be asked to imagine the tone of an oboe or the melody of "America" and respond with predetermined phrases or numbers representing the degree of vividness of the image (1). The *Farnum Music Notation Test* and the *Aliferis Music Achievement Test* are measures of another form of musical imagery.

In addition to the more conventional approaches to music testing, some experimenters have shown remarkable inventiveness in developing new procedures. Meyer, in particular, has described a unique series of testing devices identified by somewhat fanciful names, including the Tirometer, Concertometer, Rhythmometer, Hymnometer, Obe-imeter, Terpometer, and Stabilimeter (37).

GRADING

Many teachers consider the assignment of grades or marks among the most troublesome tasks they face. This is particularly true when there are large numbers of students involved and when the teacher is unable to become acquainted with the work of each pupil individually. The practice of grading is criticized on several grounds: (1) grading places too much responsibility on the teacher, (2) grades fail to reveal the causes of the success or failure they reflect, (3) they often become goals in themselves, (4) they are frequently unreliable, and (5) they reflect the quality of the teaching as much as the quality of the learning. Yet the need for evaluation has been clearly established. It is the form the evaluation is to take that remains the subject of controversy and experimentation.

One possible basis for grading is to consider each student's achievement in terms of his ability. A student who is doing the best work of which he is capable would receive a higher grade than a student who is not. Such a procedure clearly provides for individual differences, but it assumes that the teacher is able to assess accurately the ability of the student. This assessment is sometimes a source of friction with parents. Further, under this procedure a bright student may receive a "D" and a poor student may receive an "A" for the same work. Unless the system is understood by students and parents alike, the result may be confusion and resentment.

If the standards are those of the group, rather than those of the individual, there is less apparent inconsistency. The achievement of each student is compared with that of the group as a whole, and a given percentage receive "A," another percentage receive "B," and so forth, according to a curve derived arbitrarily by the teacher. The old-fashioned curve based on 10 per cent, A; 20 per cent, B; 40 per cent, C; 20 per cent, D; and 10 per cent, F, which guarantees that the students at the bottom of the scale will fail regardless of how hard they try or how much they achieve, cannot be justified in small or selective groups such as elective music classes or performance groups.

Arbitrary, fixed standards set by the teacher represent perhaps the most widely used basis for assigning grades. Under this system any number of pupils may receive "A" and any number may receive "D," depending upon actual achievement. The difficulty lies in determining just what the standards should be. Standards vary from teacher to teacher and from time to time. Also, a bright student who does not apply himself may receive the same grade as a poor student who works at the limit of his ability. The bright student has no motivation to do better, whereas the poor student may be discouraged from continuing to work at such a level.

If it is difficult to assign grades in music classes, it is even more difficult in performance groups. One major obstacle appears to be a general lack of clearly defined objective criteria for grading. Factors normally considered include effort, progress, proficiency, attitude, and attendance. The relative importance of each of these factors varies widely from one director to another, and even a single director may not weight them uniformly in grading different students. Often coupled with this lack of fixed criteria is a lack of adequate means for evaluating pupils even when criteria have been established. Proficiency in musical performance cannot be measured with the same accuracy as proficiency in other school subjects. The *Watkins-Farnum Performance Scale,* the only semi-standardized measure of performance currently available, is applicable only to band instruments and is limited as a criterion for grading. Measures of progress depend upon measures of proficiency, while effort and attitude cannot easily be measured by any objective means.

An additional complication arises from the likelihood that in large performance groups the director simply is not sufficiently familiar with the performance of each individual to evaluate him fairly. Hearing the pupil play a brief passage during rehearsal near the end of the grading period is scarcely adequate. If it is important that grades be given, it is important that they be fair and valid.

Grades in music classes and groups should be based on musical achievement and related to the musical experiences of the pupils in the classroom. The parent whose child receives an "A" in beginning band has a right to assume that his child is learning to play an instrument. The parent is justified in being indignant if he purchases an instrument on the basis of apparent accomplishment and subsequently finds that his child has no aptitude for instrumental music at all but was awarded "A's" because he tried hard or because he demonstrated a good attitude. There is no question but that a good attitude is necessary for optimum achievement. Most teachers will agree that attitude may legitimately be considered in arriving at a grade, but attitude cannot be an adequate substitute for achievement in music any more than in arithmetic or history. No arithmetic or history teacher would award an "A" on the basis of a good attitude on the part of the pupil toward the subject.

The practice of awarding grades largely on the basis of attendance, which is particularly prevalent at the college and university level, is even more difficult to justify on any philosophical basis. Neither should a student receive an "A" because he sold an unprecedented number of fruitcakes or candy bars or because he served as librarian or manager. Above all, it is particularly important that grades never be used for disciplinary purposes. Such criteria are unrelated to musical achievement.

In some elementary music programs and in some performance groups, marks of "satisfactory" or "unsatisfactory" are awarded instead of letter grades. If such marks are adequate for the purpose, this system may be practical and workable, although it constitutes avoiding the problem rather than solving it. The use of "satisfactory" and "unsatisfactory" is less feasible at the high school level, where graduation and college entrance requirements normally make letter grades mandatory. Grades expressed as percentages are still found in some schools.

Each teacher may decide for himself the criteria upon which he will grade his students, but the grade should reflect to a large extent the actual achievement of the pupil with respect to growth in music. The students and their parents should understand the basis for the grades, and there should be a consensus among the music staff of the school system on the bases for evaluation.

9

Conclusion

Testing has become a big business. Millions of tests are employed in the United States every year to measure the intelligence, aptitude, achievement, personality, and interests of citizens from the first grade through the graduate school and beyond.

OPPOSITION
TO TESTING

As long as there have been tests, there have been critics of tests. Since the 1950's, however, the critics have become more vociferous. The criticisms usually center around two major points: (1) the tests being used are inadequate and unfair, and (2) the results of testing are misunderstood and misused.

The question of the adequacy of tests is complicated by the lack of a widely accepted method of validating them. This is particularly true in music, perhaps, where the subject matter is largely of a non-quantitative nature and where there are a great many diverse and dissimilar behaviors that characterize aptitude and achievement. None of the music tests presently available is accepted universally by music educators as being entirely adequate. The question is, are any of them sufficiently adequate? It is clear that tests do not measure such factors as ambition, creativity, and imagination, though these are extremely important. It is equally clear that they may identify the talented student who does not work. The question must be answered in each specific case in the light of the accuracy required and the nature of the use to which the results are put.

No author of an aptitude test has claimed that his test measures all of the aspects of musical aptitude, or even all of the important aspects. No one is sure just what factors constitute musical aptitude or how important each is. At present we must be content to measure those which can be measured and evaluate the others by subjective means or else disregard them.

Because we cannot be sure that the factors we are measuring are indeed the important factors, we cannot be sure of the extent to which our tests are adequate. Nevertheless, the need for some means of evaluation in our music programs is unquestioned. Even though our present methods are not ideal, the substitutes we now possess, such as teacher ratings, self-ratings, and case histories, are usually less satisfactory than the objective measures we criticize.

Critics have contended that standardized tests are unfair to underprivileged children and children from minority groups. It is true that culturally deprived youngsters tend to achieve lower scores on such tests. Psychologists have replied that, if the environment of a pupil has prevented him from developing to his full potential and limited his achievement or ability relative to his middle-class peers, it is the environment rather than the test that is unfair. Because the scoring procedures are entirely objective, it is argued, such measures are more fair and more democratic than subjective measures.

There have been instances when test results have been misused. Any tool may be misused. Much of this misuse, no doubt, has stemmed from an inadequate understanding on the part of counselors, teachers, or parents as to what was being measured or how the results should be interpreted. Many of us stand in awe of the mystic power of numbers. If a counselor interprets test scores with an air of confidence and certainty, his opinions are likely to be accepted by laymen without question though they may have no sound basis. On the other hand, the more conscientious advisor who interprets scores cautiously and with numerous qualifications may be regarded as not entirely competent (9:xxiv). Of course, if a test is outdated or technically deficient, any use of it is a misuse.

Although students and parents are understandably curious about test results, a certain amount of confusion and anxiety is likely when scores are disclosed without adequate explanation of what they mean. If students are tested repeatedly and never told their scores, they are likely to become resentful, and their parents may question the time and money being spent on a testing program that produces no visible results. Parents and students have a right to be informed of test results, but the scores must be carefully interpreted for them.

Both educators and laymen have objected to the seemingly endless proliferation of tests being used. Some teachers doubt that the results derived justify the time and expense involved in administering the volume of tests currently required or expected. In many instances the examinations themselves, rather than their content, have become the objects of study. The complaint that our students are "simply tested to death" is heard with increasing frequency.

From a legal and moral viewpoint, standardized tests are often criticized as constituting an invasion of privacy. The limits beyond which a person cannot be required to divulge information about himself have not yet been established. Test results have no legal immunity from subpoena, and their confidential nature cannot be guaranteed. Though the charge of invasion of privacy has thus far been associated chiefly with personality inventories, it may also be applied to aptitude tests. Success is due to talent and hard work, but these factors are combined in vastly different ratios in different individuals. Each person should have some control over the manner in which he presents himself in the vocational marketplace, where society will decide how and whether to utilize him.

THE INFLUENCE OF TEST CONTENT ON CURRICULUM

In addition to the readily observable results of widespread testing, there are more subtle influences. Indirectly but inescapably, a testing program will exert influences that can affect the curriculum of the school. To a certain extent, the test-maker is also the curriculum-maker. The use of standardized tests, which emphasize specific blocks of subject matter, tends to establish priorities of knowledge and leads to the inevitable impression that some subjects of the curriculum are more important than others. Those subjects which are not tested come to be thought of by pupils, teachers, parents, and laymen as unimportant, although the reason for their neglect may be that we have no adequate measuring techniques.

A teacher cannot be blamed for directing his efforts toward seeing to it that his students do well on the standardized tests he knows they will be required to take. If these tests do not include music, an elementary classroom teacher, for example, is likely to neglect music in favor of other subjects in which the achievement of her pupils will be measured quantitatively in terms of the achievement of children of the same age nationally. The very lack of routine standardized tests in music tends to reduce the importance of the subject in the minds of students. However, this lack is not in itself adequate grounds for instituting or expanding a program of music testing unless the tests are sufficiently valid and useful.

DIRECTIONS FOR THE FUTURE

Probably no one test can be developed that will provide an adequate picture of an individual's aptitude or achievement, except when confined to certain limited aspects. There is likely to be more emphasis in the future upon complete batteries of tests and upon the concurrent use of dissimilar tests, with the results reported by means of profile techniques to identify specific strengths and weaknesses. There is also likely to be greater divergence between techniques designed for use with groups and techniques designed for use with individuals. Individual tests can be much more highly refined than group tests, and prognostic work for purposes of guidance is likely to be carried on increasingly under these circumstances. However, the need for group tests will remain.

In the early years of the twentieth century, music educators seeking to justify the music program in the schools usually cited the contributions of music to the so-called seven cardinal principles of education or to the four objectives of the Educational Policies Commission, or cited other non-musical or extra-musical outcomes. Now we attempt to justify the study of music primarily in terms of musical goals, and we are interested in the aesthetic values derived from the study of music more than in showing how music can contribute to an understanding of democratic processes or in teaching every fifth grader to sightread a melody by using syllables. With this change in viewpoint has come a shift in emphasis in the curriculum which, in turn, will influence achievement testing by demanding greater stress on aesthetic appreciation and insight as essential components of achievement. As a result, music tests are likely to become more musical and less atomistic.

We may also see more emphasis in the years ahead on the development of specialized tests reflecting the specialization of musicians. Further, there are some positions relating to music for which a musical background is necessary to a certain extent but for which highly developed skills of a purely musical nature are not particularly relevant. The career of the music librarian and the many types of careers in music merchandising are examples. Aptitude tests in specialized fields of music are not now imminent, but they are not beyond the realm of possibility. Such tests would have to measure a large number of closely related abilities.

Several of the improvements or developments needed in music testing are also needed in various branches of psychological testing. For example, tests are needed that are less heavily dependent upon the ability to verbalize. No test of musical aptitude can be completely adequate if it requires the student to penetrate a barrier of prerequisite verbal skills. The less such capability the student has the less valid his score will be, but the teacher has no means of determining the extent of this influence. As another example, we are urgently in need of diagnostic tests that can be used to identify the reasons for a student's failure to achieve.

The federal government has recently embarked upon a program of aid to education unprecedented in history. National concern for education has been manifested in a variety of ways, and it is now clear that the arts will no longer be so neglected as they have been in the past. Coupled with the increased spending for education at all levels, there is an increased desire to know what is being accomplished by this expenditure. For example, Title I of the Elementary and Secondary Education Act of 1965, which includes the anti-poverty provisions of the act, stipulates that all programs supported under that title be evaluated by "effective procedures, including provision for appropriate objective measurements of educational achievement" at least annually. All taxpayers share the concern of Congress for insuring that these funds are well spent. The lack of such measures in the past has served to conceal low levels of achievement, inferior standards, and ineffective teaching. However, there immediately arises the question of what measures are to be used. At present there are none in music that are clearly suitable for such purposes, although tests intended to fill closely related needs are now being developed.

SUMMARY

It is important to remember in interpreting test results that our predictions can never be perfectly accurate. In advising an individual on the basis of his test scores, there is always the possibility that we may be in error. We are unlikely ever to achieve the omniscience described facetiously by one author whereby gangsters can be sent directly to prison without waiting for them to perpetrate a single crime and diplomas and Nobel prizes can be displayed in advance on the sides of their recipients' cribs (66:114). Some individuals succeed in music, as in other fields, though all of the prognostic devices at our command indicate that they will not. This possibility cannot be ignored on the grounds that most of those who are likely to succeed can be identified. It would be tragic if a person with the potential to succeed were eliminated from the competition because of misevaluation.

Musical aptitude tests ought not to be used to exclude anyone from the best and most varied educational experiences available. Test scores cannot guarantee that the gifted student will succeed, but, when verified, they can identify the student so deficient in ability that he has little chance of success. In this sense aptitude tests may be better at predicting failure than at predicting success. The amount of time and money that can be wasted in pursuing a career under these circumstances is considerable, and the music educator has an obligation to give such a person a realistic appraisal of his chances insofar as they can be determined. This is especially true when there are other fields in which the individual appears capable of being successful. It is unfortunate that the need for guidance surpasses the adequacy of our measuring instruments. We are reasonably certain that some kinds of achievement and aptitude can be measured more or less accurately, though we recognize that others cannot. It is important in interpreting the results of measurements to realize the inherent limitations of one's tools. The use of partial and incomplete techniques cannot present a complete picture, but the test user cannot rely on the author or publisher to acquaint him with these limitations.

The enthusiasm for music testing in the 1920's and 1930's was followed by a general disenchantment from which we are only now recovering. Some of the music educators presently turning their efforts toward the construction of tests and measurements are demonstrating admirable insight and imagination. Perhaps developments in other fields, such as psychology and personnel management, will point to new directions in music testing.

The music tests we need are tests that combine, miraculously, all of the characteristics of good measuring devices. In effect, we need tests that will do all of the things we have sought to do in the past but do them better. Such utopian devices are probably even more difficult to construct than, for example, ideal tape recorders. A tape recorder should have high fidelity, yet be compact and inexpensive. We have tape recorders with fidelity so high as to be barely distinguishable from live performances. We have tape recorders so compact that they can be carried in coat pockets. We have tape recorders so inexpensive that a school can afford to place one in every classroom. But no single tape recorder combines all of these virtues. It is equally unrealistic to expect a music test to combine in itself all of the virtues expected of the ideal test.

Music testing has come a long way. Perhaps it can never be as highly developed as we would like it to be. But there is no reason to believe that it cannot be improved beyond its present state. The responsibility for improvement rests not only with test-makers but with all music educators.

Appendix

OUT-OF-PRINT MUSIC TESTS

[Note: Several well-known music tests, notably those of Lowery (30, 31), Lundin (32), Schoen (49), and Wright (69, 70), were never published separately but were described in other publications.]

Allen, Richard D., Walter H. Butterfield, and Marguerite Tully, *Providence Inventory Test in Music* (7:154). World Book Co.

Baltimore Music Achievement Test (19:1). Dept. of Music Education, Baltimore Public Schools.

Bewley, L. B., *Philippine Educational Achievement Tests: Series D, Music* (19:15). Bureau of Printing, Manila, P.I.

Bingham, W. V., *Mood Music Test* (63:622). Carnegie Institute of Technology.

Bowen, George O., *Graded Melodies for Individual Sight-Singing* (19:2). Laidlaw Brothers, New York.

Cleveland Music Test (19:2). Bureau of Educational Research, Cleveland Public Schools.

Fullerton, C. A., *Fullerton Standardized Tests in Music for Rural Schools* (19:5; 56:178). Follett Publishing Co.

Gildersleeve, Glenn, and Wayne Soper, *Musical Achievement Test* (7:154). Teachers College, Columbia University.

Gordon, Roderick D., *Gordon Index of Musical Insight* (45). By the author, Denton, Texas.

Hevner, Kate, *et al.*, *Oregon Music Tests* (21, 29). C. H. Stoelting Co., Chicago.

Hillbrand, E. K., *Hillbrand Sight-Singing Test* (7:151). World Book Co.

Hutchinson, Herbert, and L. C. Pressey, *Hutchinson Music Tests* (19:7). Public School Publishing Co., Bloomington, Ill.

Kelsey, Julia R., *Kelsey Standardized Tests of Musical Accomplishment* (19:7). C. A. Gregory Co., Cincinnati.

Kotick, M. Lela, and T. L. Torgerson, *Diagnostic Tests of Achievement in Music* (6:340). California Test Bureau.

Krone, Max T., *Krone Tonal Dictation Test, Krone Recognition Test, Krone Rhythmic Dictation Test* (19:8-9). Bureau of Educational Research, Cleveland Public Schools.

McCauley, Clara J., *McCauley Examination in Public School Music* (7:153). Joseph E. Avent, Knoxville.

McDade, James E., *Plymouth Educational Tests: No. 100A, Key Signatures* (19:15). Plymouth Press, Chicago.

Moon, Doris, *Moon Diagnostic Tests in Harmony* (19:13). L. R. Jones, Los Angeles.

Musical Appreciation Ability Test (8:120). Robert Gibson Sons, Glasgow, Scotland.

Otterstein, Adolph W., and Raymond M. Mosher, *O-M Sight-Singing Test* (19:14). Stanford University Press.

Petry, Harriet, and Marie Rasey, *Courtis Standard Research Tests: Series M, Music* ("Recognition of Characteristic Rhythms" and "Recognition of Mood from Melody") (18:160-161; 19:2). S. A. Courtis, Detroit.

Philadelphia Test in Music Information (64:204-5). Board of Education, Philadelphia.

Schultz, E. J., *Schultz Test of Listening Power in Music* (19:16; 50). E. J. Schultz, Tucson.

Seltzer, Seraphine S., *A Measure of Singing and Rhythmic Development of Preschool Children* (54). Merrill-Palmer School, Detroit.

Taylor, C. K., *Taylor Music Test* (19:19). Schola Press, New York.

Tinker, M. A., *Self-Ratings in Music* (63:475). C. H. Stoelting Co., Chicago.

Torgerson, T. L., and Ernest Fahnestock, *Torgerson-Fahnestock Music Test* (19:19). Public School Publishing Co., Bloomington, Ill.

Whistler, Harvey S., and Louis P. Thorpe, *Musical Aptitude Test* (5:384). California Test Bureau.

Wood, C. P., *Ear Tests in Harmony* (8:119). American Book Co.

REFERENCES

1. Agnew, Marie, "A Comparison of the Auditory Images of Musicians, Psychologists and Children," *Psychological Monographs*, XXXI (1922), 268-278.

2. Bentley, Arnold, *Musical Ability in Children and Its Measurement*. New York: October House, 1966.

3. Bower, Libbie B., *A Factor Analysis of Music Tests*. Washington: Catholic University of America Press, 1945.

4. Brown, Andrew W., "The Reliability and Validity of the Seashore Tests of Musical Talent," *Journal of Applied Psychology*, XII (1928), 468-476.
5. Buros, Oscar K., ed., *The Fifth Mental Measurements Yearbook*. Highland Park, N.J.: The Gryphon Press, 1959.
6. ———, ed., *The Fourth Mental Measurements Yearbook*. Highland Park, N.J., The Gryphon Press, 1953.
7. ———, ed., *The Nineteen Forty Mental Measurements Yearbook*. Highland Park, N.J.: The Mental Measurements Yearbook, 1941.
8. ———, ed., *The Nineteen Thirty-Eight Mental Measurements Yearbook*. New Brunswick, N.J.: Rutgers University Press, 1938.
9. ———, ed., *Tests in Print*. Highland Park, N.J.: The Gryphon Press, 1961.
10. Dexter, Emily S., and Katharine T. Omwake, "The Relation Between Pitch Discrimination and Accent in Modern Languages," *J. Appl. Psych.*, XVIII (1934), 267-271.
11. Drake, Raleigh M., "Factorial Analysis of Music Tests by the Spearman Tetrad-Difference Technique," *Journal of Musicology*, I (1939), 6-16.
12. ———, "The Validity and Reliability of Tests of Musical Talent," *J. Appl. Psych.*, XVII (1933), 447-458.
13. Edmondson, Harold S., "The *Seashore Measures of Musical Talents* as a Prognostic Guide in Language Rehabilitation for Persons with Aphasia." Unpublished Ph.D. dissertation, University of Michigan, 1954.
14. Educational Council [Music Education Research Council], "A Standard Course in Music," Music Educators National Conference *Journal of Proceedings*, 1921, pp. 220-231.
15. Farnsworth, Paul R., "An Historical, Critical, and Experimental Study of the Seashore-Kwalwasser Test Battery," *Genetic Psychology Monographs*, IX (1931), 291-393.
16. ———, *Musical Taste: Its Measurement and Cultural Nature*. Stanford, Calif.: Stanford University Press, 1950.
17. ———, "Rating Scales for Musical Interests," *Journal of Psychology*, XXVIII (1949), 245-253.
18. ———, *The Social Psychology of Music*. New York: Holt, Rinehart & Winston, Inc., 1958.
19. Flemming, Cecile W., and Marion Flagg, *A Descriptive Bibliography of Prognostic and Achievement Tests in Music*. New York: Teachers College, Columbia University, 1936.
20. Garrett, Henry E., *Statistics in Psychology and Education*, 5th ed. New York: David McKay Co., Inc., 1958.
21. Hevner, Kate, "Appreciation of Music and Tests for the Appreciation of Music," *Studies in Appreciation of Art (University of Oregon Publication*, IV, 6 [1934]), 83-151.
22. Highsmith, J. A., "Selecting Musical Talent," *J. Appl. Psych.*, XIII (1929), 486-493.
23. Karlin, J. E., "A Factorial Study of Auditory Function," *Psychometrika*, VII (1942), 251-279.
24. Kuo, Ping Wen, *The Chinese System of Public Education*. Contributions to Education, No. 64. New York: Teachers College, Columbia University, 1915.
25. Kwalwasser, Jacob, *Exploring the Musical Mind*. New York: Coleman-Ross, 1955.
26. Lamp, Charles J., and Noel Keys, "Can Aptitude for Specific Musical Instruments Be Predicted?" *Journal of Educational Psychology*, XXVI (1935), 587-596.
27. Larson, Ruth C., "Finding and Guiding Musical Talent," *Music Educators Journal*, XLII, 1 (1955), 22-25.

28. ———, *Studies on Seashore's Measures of Musical Talent*. University of Iowa Studies: Series on Aims and Progress of Research, No. 174. Iowa City: University of Iowa, 1930.

29. Long, Newell, "A Revision of the University of Oregon Music Discrimination Test." Unpublished Ed.D. dissertation, Indiana University, 1965.

30. Lowery, Harry, "Cadence and Phrase Tests in Music," *British Journal of Psychology*, XVII (1926-1927), 111-118.

31. ———, "Musical Memory," *Brit. J. Psych.*, XIX (1928-1929), 397-404.

32. Lundin, Robert W., "The Development and Validation of a Set of Musical Ability Tests," *Psych. Monog.* LXIII (1949), 1-20.

33. ———, *An Objective Psychology of Music*. New York: The Ronald Press Company, 1953.

34. McGinnis, Esther, "Seashore's Measures of Musical Ability Applied to Children of the Pre-School Age," *American Journal of Psychology*, XL (1928), 620-623.

35. McLeish, John, "The Validation of Seashore's Measures of Musical Talent by Factorial Methods," *Brit. J. Psych. Statistical Section*, III (1950), 129-140.

36. Merry, Ralph V., "Adapting the Seashore Musical Talent Tests for Use with Blind Pupils," *Teachers Forum*, III, 4 (1931), 15-19.

37. Meyer, Max F., "Special Ability Tests as Used in Missouri; Including a Demonstration of a Typical Test," *Psychological Bulletin*, XXI (1924), 114-116.

38. More, Grace Van Dyke, "Prognostic Testing in Music on the College Level," *Journal of Educational Research*, XXVI (1932), 199-212.

39. Mosher, Raymond M., *A Study of Group Method of Measurement of Sight-Singing*. Contributions to Education, No. 194. New York: Teachers College, Columbia University, 1925.

40. Mueller, Kate Hevner, "Studies in Music Appreciation," *Journal of Research in Music Education*, IV (1956), 3-25.

41. Mursell, James L., "Measuring Musical Ability and Achievement," *J. Ed. Res.*, XXV (1932), 116-126.

42. ———, *The Psychology of Music*. New York: W. W. Norton & Company, Inc., 1937.

43. ———, "What About Music Tests?" *Mus. Ed. J.*, XXIV, 2 (1937), 16-18.

44. National Interscholastic Music Activities Commission, *NIMAC Manual*. Washington: Music Educators National Conference, 1963.

45. Perry, William W., "A Comparative Study of Selected Tests for Predicting Proficiency in Collegiate Music Theory." Unpublished Ed.D. dissertation, North Texas State University, 1965.

46. Ream, Merrill J., "The Tapping Test: A Measure of Motility," *Psych. Monog.*, XXXI (1922), 293-319.

47. Saetveit, Joseph G., Don Lewis, and Carl E. Seashore, *Revision of the Seashore Measures of Musical Talents*. University of Iowa Studies: Series on Aims and Progress of Research, No. 338. Iowa City: University of Iowa, 1940.

48. Schoen, Max, *The Psychology of Music*. New York: The Ronald Press Company, 1940.

49. ———, "Tests of Musical Feeling and Musical Understanding," *Journal of Comparative Psychology*, V (1925), 31-52.

50. Schultz, E. J., "Testing Listening Power in Music," *Music Educators National Conference Yearbook*, 1933, pp. 306-312.

51. Seashore, Carl E., *Psychology of Music*. New York: McGraw-Hill Book Company, 1938.

52. ———, *The Psychology of Musical Talent*. Morristown, N.J.: Silver Burdett Company, 1919.

53. Seashore, Robert H., "Improvability in Pitch Discrimination," *Psych. Bull.*, XXXII (1935), 545.

54. Seltzer, Seraphine S., "A Measure of the Singing and Rhythmic Development of Preschool Children," *J. Ed. Psych.*, XXVII (1936), 417-424.

55. Smith, Franklin O., "The Effect of Training in Pitch Discrimination," *Psych. Monog.*, XVI (1914), 67-103.

56. Smith, Henry L., and Wendell W. Wright, *Second Revision of the Bibliography of Educational Measurements* (*Bulletin of the School of Education, Indiana University*, IV, 2 [1927]).

57. Stanton, Hazel M., *Measurement of Musical Talent: The Eastman Experiment*. University of Iowa Studies in the Psychology of Music, II. Iowa City: University of Iowa, 1935.

58. Stanton, Hazel M., and Wilhelmine Koerth, *Musical Capacity Measures of Adults Repeated After Music Education*. University of Iowa Studies: Series on Aims and Progress of Research, No. 189. Iowa City: University of Iowa, 1930.

59. ———, *Musical Capacity Measures of Children Repeated After Musical Training*. University of Iowa Studies: Series on Aims and Progress of Research, No. 259. Iowa City: University of Iowa, 1933.

60. Taylor, Elizabeth M., "A Study in the Prognosis of Musical Talent," *Journal of Experimental Education*, X (1941), 1-28.

61. Tilson, Lowell M., "A Study of the Prognostic Value of the Tilson-Gretsch Test for Musical Aptitude," *Teachers College Journal*, XII (1940-1941), 110-112.

62. Travis, Lee E., and Mildred G. Davis, "The Relation Between Faulty Speech and Lack of Certain Musical Talents," *Psych. Monog.*, XXXVI (1926-1927), 71-81.

63. Wang, Charles K. A., *An Annotated Bibliography of Mental Tests and Scales*. Vol. I. Peiping, China. Catholic University Press, 1939.

64. ———, *An Annotated Bibliography of Mental Tests and Scales*. Vol. II. Peiping, China. Catholic University Press, 1940.

65. Watkins, John G., *Objective Measurement of Instrumental Performance*. Contributions to Education, No. 860. New York: Teachers College, Columbia University, 1942.

66. Wernick, Robert, *They've Got Your Number*. New York: W. W. Norton & Company, Inc., 1956.

67. Wing, Herbert D., "A Factorial Study of Musical Tests," *Brit. J. Psych.*, XXXI (1940-1941), 341-355.

68. Woody, Clifford, *Standardized Tests Designed for Use in Institutions of Higher Learning*. Washington: American Council on Education, 1930.

69. Wright, Frances A., "The Correlation Between Achievement and Capacity in Music," *J. Ed. Res.*, XVII (1928), 50-56.

70. ———, "The Relation of Music Endowment and Achievement Tests to Teacher Selection," *MENC J. Proc.*, 1928, pp. 289-301.

71. Wyatt, Ruth F., "Improvability of Pitch Discrimination," *Psych. Monog.*, LVIII (1945), 1-58.

Index